Dominik P. Matyka et al.

Company Success among German Internet Start-ups

Social Media, Investors
and Entrepreneurs' Personalities

disserta
Verlag

Matyka, Dominik P. et al.: Company Success among German Internet Start-ups: Social
Media, Investors and Entrepreneurs' Personalities, Hamburg, disserta Verlag, 2012

Dissertation Technische Universität Berlin, 2011

ISBN: 978-3-95425-066-0
Druck: disserta Verlag, Hamburg, 2012

Covermotiv: istockphoto.com/VikaSuh
Covergestaltung: Sabine Zug (www.plista.com)

Bibliografische Information der Deutschen Nationalbibliothek
Die Deutsche Nationalbibliothek verzeichnet diese Publikation in der Deutschen
Nationalbibliografie; detaillierte bibliografische Daten sind im Internet über
http://dnb.d-nb.de abrufbar.

Die digitale Ausgabe (Ebook-Ausgabe) dieses Titels trägt die ISBN 978-3-95425-067-7
und kann über den Handel oder den Verlag bezogen werden.

Published by disserta Verlag, Hamburg, Germany, 2012
All rights reserved. No part of this work may be used or reproduced in any manner
whatsoever without written permission except in the case of brief quotations embodied in
published reviews of the book.

Dieses Werk ist urheberrechtlich geschützt. Die dadurch begründeten Rechte,
insbesondere die der Übersetzung, des Nachdrucks, des Vortrags, der Entnahme von
Abbildungen und Tabellen, der Funksendung, der Mikroverfilmung oder der
Vervielfältigung auf anderen Wegen und der Speicherung in Datenverarbeitungsanlagen,
bleiben, auch bei nur auszugsweiser Verwertung, vorbehalten. Eine Vervielfältigung
dieses Werkes oder von Teilen dieses Werkes ist auch im Einzelfall nur in den Grenzen
der gesetzlichen Bestimmungen des Urheberrechtsgesetzes der Bundesrepublik
Deutschland in der jeweils geltenden Fassung zulässig. Sie ist grundsätzlich
vergütungspflichtig. Zuwiderhandlungen unterliegen den Strafbestimmungen des
Urheberrechtes.

Die Wiedergabe von Gebrauchsnamen, Handelsnamen, Warenbezeichnungen usw. in
diesem Werk berechtigt auch ohne besondere Kennzeichnung nicht zu der Annahme,
dass solche Namen im Sinne der Warenzeichen- und Markenschutz-Gesetzgebung als frei
zu betrachten wären und daher von jedermann benutzt werden dürften.

Die Informationen in diesem Werk wurden mit Sorgfalt erarbeitet. Dennoch können
Fehler nicht vollständig ausgeschlossen werden und der Verlag, die Autoren oder
Übersetzer übernehmen keine juristische Verantwortung oder irgendeine Haftung für evtl.
verbliebene fehlerhafte Angaben und deren Folgen.

© disserta Verlag, ein Imprint der Diplomica Verlag GmbH
http://www.disserta-verlag.de, Hamburg 2012
Hergestellt in Deutschland

Preface

There has been a lot of research on factors that help to explain why some start-ups become successful and their founders rich, and on the other hand why other start-ups fail terribly. Of course, starting up an enterprise is a complex activity dependent on institutional regulations, competitors, market developments and the simple recognition of the right opportunities at the right time. We know all of this, but still cannot accurately predict our chances of being successful as entrepreneur. There are some methods venture capitalists use, such as evaluating start-up teams and studying business plans. However, even after doing this, the chance of making a correct prediction is still lower than throwing a coin. Research has never been able to explain much of this complexity, but there are at least three factors that have repeatedly turned up when determining success and failure in the last few years.

The first of these factors is a result of our tremendous technological development in the past few decades, but particularly in the most recent. In nearly all young enterprises, the utilization of social media and social networks has become a vital factor for survival and success. Many research results over the last few years have yielded the conclusion that social media are by far the most important platform for marketing products and services. To put this more scientifically, the diffusion of innovation is increasingly interlinked with social media. In addition, the recognition and creation of opportunities also increasingly requires social media platforms. However, this does not mean one should operate only online, investing all of his time and energy to communicating in social networks.

The second factor concerns something that is quite obvious: money. Since the vast majority of start-ups do not have their own money or the ability to easily get a loan, obtaining financial resources is often a major problem. There are different ways to raise some money: One can ask friends and family, fool others, or even rob banks, but often the only course of action is to be financed by venture capital. But how do start-ups find the right venture capital investor, and how much does this investor intervene in the start-up's management? All this can be answered by looking at the social networks of venture capitalists and young enterprises.

The third factor depends partially on the first. Before the development of online social media, founders may have been described as extroverted, aggressive and emotionally stable. However, within social media these characteristics often disappear to a certain degree, creating a sort of anonymity. If this is correct, we must rethink the search for personnel, the composition of a start-up's team, and even the evaluation of start-ups in pitches. Technical development has indeed made it possible for introverted nerds to be more successful than extroverted offliners. Historically, what are considered successful characteristics has changed several times, and it is important to know whether the current technological development will again trigger such changes.

This book, presented in three essays, gathers up the threads and attempts to shed light on all three factors. As you will read, spending more time and energy in online activities does not make you more successful as entrepreneur. However, spending no time at all also does not make you more successful—spending energy and time wisely is the key. Moreover, networking has become a buzzword, but it would appear nobody actually knows how to do this, except by distributing as many business cards as possible or piling up more and more friends on social networks. This book shows how networks of investors and start-ups are structured towards success. And finally, though it may be hard to believe, we have broken down the personality traits of successful entrepreneurs. This book is one of the first to identify and explain this twist.

About the Author

Dr. Dominik P. Matyka (1982) studied International Business Studies at the University of Vienna, Cass Business School London, the University of St. Gallen and at the Technical University of Berlin. In 2008, he founded plista GmbH, an online and mobile recommendation and ad network for text/image and video ad formats. As CEO for plista, Dr. Matyka is responsible for Marketing, Sales and Investor/Partner Relations.

Prior to this, Dr. Matyka had co-founded several different start-ups (including youmix GmbH and HiClip GmbH), focusing on sales and business development. In addition, Dr. Matyka is involved in Business Angel Investments (apprupt, eFamous, and SiRank amongst others) through his role as CEO of u25 Ventures GmbH, and is a founding partner and early stage-investor of Linden Ventures (http://lindenvc.com).

Company Success among German Internet Start-ups

1 Overview 1

2 Analysis of perceived importance, objective usage patterns and effienciency of social media activities among German Internet and technology start-up companies 30

3 It is not only the investors' network, but the frequency of interaction between investors and founders that drives the performance of start-up companies 70

4 Unsealing the relationship between entrepreneurs' success and their personality in the advent of web 2.0 98

Table of Contents

1.1 Motivation and Contribution 1
1.2 Summary and Implication 5
    1.2.1 Analysis of perceived importance, objective usage patterns and efficiency of social media activities among German Internet and technology start-up companies 5
    1.2.2 It is not only the investors' network, but the frequency of interaction between investors and founders that drives the performance of start-up companies 7
    1.2.3 Unsealing the relationship between entrepreneurs' success and their personality in the advent of web 2.0 10
Bibliography 14

2 Analysis of perceived importance, objective usage patterns and efficiency of social media activities among German Internet and technology start-up companies 30
2.1 Introduction 31
2.2 Literature review and theoretical background 33
    2.2.1 Introduction to social media 33
    2.2.2 Social media landscape 33
    2.2.3 Start-up companies as object of investigation 35
    2.2.4 How to embrace return-on-investment in online marketing, especially social media 36
2.3 Methodology 38
    2.3.1 Research Design 39
    2.3.2 Sample 43
    2.3.3 Procedure 45
    2.3.4 Measurement instruments 46

2.4   Results 48
    2.4.1   Descriptives 48
    2.4.2   The importance of social media platforms 49
    2.4.3   The usage of social media according to the perceived importance .. 50
    2.4.4   The usage of social media and financial success 53
2.5   Discussion 59
    2.5.1   Limitations 61
    2.5.2   Future Research 63
Bibliography 65

3   It is not only the investors' network, but the frequency of interaction between investors and founders that drives the performance of start-up companies 70
3.1   Introduction 71
3.2   Literature Review and Hypothesis 73
3.3   Research Methodology 79
    3.3.1   Sample 80
    3.3.2   Operationalization 82
3.4   Results 85
3.5   Discussion and Conclusion 89
    3.5.1   Limitations 90
    3.5.2   Future Research 90
Vita Co-Author Stephan Jung 92
Bibliography 93

4   Unsealing the relationship between entrepreneurs' success and their personality in the advent of web 2.0 98
4.1   Introduction 98
4.2   Theoretical and operational framework 100
4.3   Hypotheses 103

4.4	Method	108
	4.4.1 Sample	108
	4.4.2 Measuring Personal Traits	109
	4.4.3 Social Media Usage	111
	4.4.4 Entrepreneurial Performance	112
	4.4.5 Analytical Techniques	114
4.5	Results	116
4.6	Discussion and Conclusions	120
Vita Co-Author Jan Kratzer		123
Bibliography		124

Overview

1.1 Motivation and Contribution

Creating new businesses by exploring new and innovative ideas produces economic growth (Schumpeter, 1942). Start-up companies require access to a range of resources, including capital (Smith, 2009). Aside from financial resources, marketing is widely considered as an important success factor for companies of all stages and sizes. Several authors point out that „entrepreneurial marketing should have a special impact on new ventures' success" (Gruber, 2005; Schulte, 2010). Entrepreneurship and marketing therefore become „intersected," while „successful entrepreneurs practice marketing and the better marketers act entrepreneurial" (Day et al., 1998; Hills et al., 2010). Further, Hills points out that business owners nowadays tend to be more customer-driven (2010) and social media clearly provides the means to act this way.

At the heart of entrepreneurial business several ingredients have proven to facilitate a crucial impact on success. Our research focuses on three of them: (a) the relationship between social media and business success, (b) investors' network positions and the entrepreneurs' frequency of interaction with them, and (c) entrepreneurs' personality traits in the advent of web 2.0.

Out of several requirements, we have chosen the Internet industry in Germany as an empirical setting. Our initial data sample consists of over 900 Internet and technology start-up companies, founded from January 2005 until December 2009, and is demographically diverse. We decided to research this industry as we assume that social media is a technology-driven innovation and Internet companies are among the first to adapt to those new media tools (relevant for paper 1 and 3). Furthermore, the sample is large and diverse enough to analyze syndication networks of investors among a rather young industry where relationships between investors and entrepreneurs can be easily tracked (relevant for paper 2). As no databases comparable to US-based VentureOne or VentureSource exist in Germany, public databases available on German entrepreneur-focused websites such as www.deutsche-startups.de and www.gruenderszene.de were used for data collection, assuming that start-up companies not being mentioned there have not yet overcome the hurdle of raising general interest and lack clear visibility on the Internet. The German Handelsregister (commercial register) was used to extract information on syndication networks formed by investors and were manually crosschecked through publicly available sources on diverse venture capital databases and venture capital web sites. Founding management was selected as addressee to ensure qualified answers with regard to certain financial question in the survey, which took place from March through July 2010. A complementary explanatory website was put online to ensure positive feedback.

As we did not have any access to data on the actual usage of social media through the questionnaire, we used in-depth crawling and data mining techniques with self-developed algorithms to capture social media behaviour. To ensure a non-biased answering of questions, the start-up founders were not informed beforehand about the screening and capturing of their social media behaviour. During a one-month period from July 2010 to August 2010, the social media platforms Twitter and Facebook were crawled and manual research on the companies' corporate websites and using Weblog search engines was done to analyze blogging behaviour. Blogging usage was analyzed by investigating the amount of Weblog postings over a period of 12 months. We analyzed Twitter usage patterns by counting the amount of followers gained as a result of usage or engagement. Facebook, due to its restrictiveness and data closeness, was just measured by counting the amount of fans gained, in absolute numbers. Although we are aware that Twitter and Facebook were not measured directly by their usage or activity (e.g. through messages posted) but rather by their results, we believe that usage patterns are nevertheless directly correlated to the followers and fans gained.

Entrepreneurial success can be tied to different parameters. Oftentimes statistical models of financial characteristics of established companies are used as success determinants (Keasey and Watson, 1991). Indicators include firm survival (e.g. Ciaverella et al., 2004), growth (e.g. Lee and Tsang, 2001) and economic indicators such as profitability (Zhao et al., 2010). Since common financial performance indicators such as sales, return on investment and profits are not easily available from start-up companies (Baumann et al., 2000), we decided to follow an alternative approach by using other variables that represent economic performance of a start-up. According to McDougall et al. (1992), those variables can be divided into two general groups, namely objective and subjective measurements. According to Baumann et al. (2004), objective measures of start-up success include the growth of the organization; organizational growth is also represented through growth of the number of employees, which in our case is used as an appropriate alternative measure for objective performance. Subjective performance measures consist of variables that were measured through self-evaluating performance on internal development. To evaluate internal performance, founding management was asked to describe the status of their start-ups' revenue situations. The number of customers, in comparison to a start-up's strongest domestic and international competitor, was also used as a success indicator.

Alongside these variables, such as the revenue dimension – which is one of the most mentioned success indicators (Murphy et al., 1996) – the degree of financing, according to Whippler (1998), represents another very important input factor for assessing start-ups' success. To overcome the gap on financial data of non-listed companies, the start-ups were asked to expose their financial structure. The goal was not to show different rounds of financing received by start-ups but rather to identify total cash received, a measure that shows the start-ups' attractiveness and therefore is believed to be a success indicator. Based on a comparison to a company's financial stock value, we developed a variable that reflects the capital infusion received by start-ups, the so-called financial value variable (FVV). Where appropriate, different success scales were finally integrated into one scale and combined with the financial value variable into one scale of entrepreneurial performance.

Figure 1: Derivation of the financial value variable (FVV)

Degree of financing	*Financial value variable (FVV)*
Start-ups that received at least family & friends investment or used own cash	1
Start-ups that received at least one business angel round	2
Start-ups that received one venture capital round	3
Start-ups that received a family & friends or business angel round and at least one venture capital round	4
Start-ups that received several venture capital rounds	5

Cash investments into a start-up company seem to us a legitimate indicator for performance because if investors are willing to invest in a company, it stands to reason that the respective company already performs well; because of that, we believe the Financial Value Variable to be an appropriate measurement dimension.

In sum, our research, which is based on three papers represented in chapters 2, 3, and 4, addressed different fields of entrepreneurial success determinants.

1. What is the relationship between social media perception, actual usage, and start-up success?
2. What are the effects of a start-up company's investors' position within a syndication network and the performance of the investor's fund, respectively, on the start-up's success?
3. Do certain personality traits of start-up entrepreneurs lead to higher social media usage, and in what way are any personality characteristics affecting start-ups' success?

We believe the results to be of explorative nature to some extent, and further research is needed.

1.2 Summary and Implication

1.2.1 Analysis of perceived importance, objective usage patterns and efficiency of social media activities among German Internet and technology start-up companies

The objective of the first paper (chapter 2) is to drive evidence to the correlation of social media usage and start-up companies' success. We find out that approximately every second technology-driven start-up values at least one social media platform as being very important for its strategic objectives (47.9%), and thus implements at least some adequate usage patterns. However, social media proves not to be positively correlated with a start-up's financial success. To the contrary, the study shows that the stronger the financial stability of start-ups, the less they tend to use social media.

Three propositions were formulated to empirically explore the above-described objective. A web-based survey, asking start-ups' founding management executives for the general subjective importance of Facebook, Twitter and corporate Weblogs with regard to the company's strategic and marketing objectives, was conducted to test the platforms' perceived importance from the company's own perspective. An analysis of numerous usage patterns of social media addressed the second proposition of testing perceived importance of those media according to their usage. Lastly, start-ups were asked to describe their financial status and financing degree; theses financial indicators were taken to be synonymous with a company's success.

The results show that 86.7% of the surveyed start-ups value at least one social media platform as important for their strategic marketing objectives, with social networks such as Facebook the most important (40.55%). Further, 94.49% of all start-ups claimed to have high knowledge in at least one platform. Tested through a Chi-Square statistical test ($p < .05$), a statistically significant relationship of social media importance and social media knowledge was revealed. Although general importance of those platforms was found to be crucially important for success, usage patterns differed widely, with just 65.13% of the start-ups interviewed using a corporate Weblog, 52.99% maintaining a corporate Twitter account and only 41.93% being active with a corporate Facebook page. We then correlated the importance and frequency of usage of those platforms and tested their relationship as being statistically significant, applying a Chi-Square statistical test ($p < .05$). The results show that start-up companies tend to implement the right social media strategies based on their importance evaluation, i.e. the more important a social media platform becomes, the higher its usage. A similar relationship between knowledge of social media and its usage can be observed. Financial success was analyzed by evaluating the revenue situation of the sampled start-ups, with 9.17% of the whole sample not generating any revenues at all, 51.83% having proved to generate at least first revenues, having already launched their services to the public, and only 17.43% to be cash-flow break-even. A second financial parameter was introduced, and analyzed the types of external financing rounds received; it was assumed that the more financing a start-up receives the more attractive it is to investors, and that this therefore shows another dimension of start-up success (based on the ability to attract venture capital). The revenue situation and financial value (measured in financing received) were used as success dimensions to be then correlated to importance and usage levels of social media. Central findings of this study are:

1. Social media is perceived to be generally important by almost 90% of all German Internet start-ups.
2. Approximately eight out of ten start-ups use social media regularly, with Facebook and Twitter being the most important platforms.
3. A high synchronism between perceived importance of social media and actual usage can be observed.
4. Start-ups that perceive social media to be important are at least as successful as start-ups that actually use social media extensively.
5. There is a tendency that start-ups decrease social media usage once becoming financially stable.

1.2.2 It is not only the investors' network, but the frequency of interaction between investors and founders that drives the performance of start-up companies

The second paper (chapter 3) mainly addresses the research questions (a) to what extent the position of an investor in a syndication network influences start-ups' success and (b) to what extent the frequency of interaction between founders and investors affects this relationship. Hence, we depict the effects of a start-up company's investors' position within a syndication network and the performance of their fund. Syndication networks are networks of venture capitalists, forming to conjointly invest or co-invest in companies, and therefore sharing risks and obtaining diverse information and knowledge (Bygrave, 1987). The frequency of interaction between founders and investors was found to be an influencing factor on the start-up's performance. Our research results show that the better the network position of the lead investor is within the syndication network, the better the performance of it. Further, we see that even without taking the network position of the investor into account, a higher rate of communication and interaction between founders and investors helps in performance output. It can be concluded that it is not only the quality of the investors' network a founder should look at when searching for funding, but also the investment strategy of the investor in terms of time allocated to his portfolio.

Aside from a founder's idea, capital is an important factor for success (Gompers and Lerner, 2001). Therefore, our study focused on the investor networks' impact on start-ups, proposing that accessibility to a network is as important as its quality. Research showed that the ability to establish ties with venture capitalists positively correlates with the ability to attract venture capital (Shane and Stuart, 2002); due to the fact that investors follow different investment strategies in regards to time allocated to their portfolio companies, these companies can only make use of their investors' network according to the extent they gain access to this network.

Our research approach is twofold. First, we did a social network analysis (SNA) of all German investors investing in Internet start-ups at the end of 2009, based on all deals these investors closed since 2005, using SNA software UCInet. Second, we concluded a web-based questionnaire, asking all those start-ups' founding management to disclose their time investment with their investor. Within the SNA, the measures „centrality" and „betweenness" are used as variables that show the quality of the syndication network a start-up has access to (Hochberg et al., 2007)—the first measure exposing the network position of an actor in relation to other network actors and the latter measuring the proportion of all paths linking actors that are connected through this particular investor. The frequency of interaction was measured by asking the founders about the frequency of face-to-face and virtual communication with the lead-investor. The mean was one interaction per month on average. Company performance variables included objective and subjective performance measurements (e.g. McDougall et al., 1992). The objective measure was growth of the number of employees (average: 2.3) as appropriate alternative indicator (Baumann et al., 2004) and subjective performance measures included a self-evaluation on internal development in terms of the current revenue situation (most companies are on their way to break-even). Control variables included founders' education, age and experience.

Our results are based on two different models we calculated, one with the dependant variable measuring objective performance of the start-ups, and the other based on the subjective dependent variable to proof the results of the main regression analysis. Because of its nominal scale, multinominal logit regression model (FcFadden, 1982) was used for the analysis of the dependant variable *subjective performance* and linear regression analysis for the dependant variable *objective performance*. Throughout each model we found significant positive effects of the network position of an investor on the performance of their portfolio. Second, we conclude that even without taking the network position of the investor into account, a higher rate of communication between founders and investors helps start-up companies to outperform. And lastly, this latter effect lowers and is no longer significant when analyzing the mediator effect of the frequency of interaction.

1.2.3 Unsealing the relationship between entrepreneurs' success and their personality in the advent of web 2.0

The objective of the third paper (Chapter 4) is to enhance the understanding of the relationship between entrepreneurs' success and their personalities in the advent of web 2.0 applications. We investigate this relationship by taking the impact of entrepreneurs utilizing web 2.0 platforms into account and the mediating and moderating role of personal traits on web 2.0 usage. The findings of our research show that the personality traits Extraversion and Emotional Stability have a direct and positive impact on business performance, in the same way as the usage of social media tools such as Twitter and Facebook increases it. We conclude our research by detecting moderating effects of the personality traits Extraversion, Emotional Stability and to some degree Agreeableness to the usage of web 2.0 technology and business success. We focus on answering the question whether entrepreneurs under the current state of personality do or do not have appropriate aptitudes for business success in the light of social media usage.

Several studies (e.g. Bear et al., 2008; Costello and Hodson, 2010) show that the 10-item Personality Inventory Measure (TIPI) gives adequate and stable results when investigating entrepreneurial characteristics. TIPI is based on five basic dimensions of human personality, i.e. Openness, Conscientiousness, Extraversion, Agreeableness and Emotional Stability (Gosling et al., 2003). In our research, a company's success is exclusively indicated through growth numbers (e.g. number of customers) and the magnitude of venture capital that has been received (Whippler, 1998). We assume a direct relationship between certain personality traits and entrepreneurial success and between social media usage and business performance. In the latter relationship we further propose mediating effects between certain personality traits and business performance, stating that certain effects are weakened, strengthened, appearing or disappearing when considering personal traits in the relationship of social media and company success; lastly, we expect moderating effects between social media usage, personality traits and entrepreneurial success.

Through a web-based survey, entrepreneurs from the German technology landscape with companies founded between 2005 and 2009 were asked to indicate the extent to which they agree or disagree to the 10-item scale of TIPI. Social media usage data was gathered through in-depth crawling algorithms and datamining techniques. Entrepreneurial performance as variable was formed through an integration of multiple scales such as number of customers in relation to German and international competitors through self-assessment along a 5-point Likert scale and diverse economic scales such as revenue dimension and a financial value variable, which shows the different types of external capital received.

Latent class regression analysis was applied to test the hypotheses and 2-log Likelihood, and the Bayesian Information Criterion and overall R^2 were used as proxy for explaining the variance. Both mediation and moderation hypotheses were tested with latent class regression analysis, following Baron and Kenny (1986). Residual plots and collinearity diagnostics were examined before conducting regression analysis. Variables on personality traits were included in the model and contrasted with the no-predictor model. In a second step, variables on social media were included. And lastly, the variables on social media plus the variables on personality traits were put together to examine mediating effects respectively, molded to test for moderating effects.

Several authors (e.g. Ross et al., 2009; Landers and Lounsbury, 2006) point out that social media usage may be personality dependent and that certain traits may stimulate the efficient usage of it and certain not. We find that Blog usage positively correlates with Twitter usage (0.12%) and Facebook usage (0.23%). Further, correlations between personality traits and social media only show a weak to medium strength. Emotional Stability and Extraversion as variables correlate positively with Twitter (0.13% and 0.11%, respectively) and Facebook (0.14% and 0.13%, respectively) usage, however Openness correlates negatively (-0.29% and -0.12%, respectively). Openness further has a negative sign concerning the correlation with Extraversion (-0.62%). Lastly, we conclude that the variable Entrepreneurial Performance is positively impacted by the entrepreneur's trait Emotional Stability (0.17%) and by Twitter and Facebook usage (0.12% and 0.14%, respectively) on a statistically significant level ($p < .05$).

Latent class regression was used to examine the influence of personality characteristics on entrepreneurs' performance. We concluded that Emotional Stability positively determines Entrepreneurial Performance; likewise, Twitter and Facebook usage as well as the character trait Extraversion impact Entrepreneurial Performance positively on a statistically significant level. A first model using latent class regression to test mediating effects of entrepreneurial traits on the usage of Facebook and Twitter shows that the effect of Twitter usage loses statistical significance, the effect of the variable Emotional Stability becomes larger, and the effects of the variables Extraversion and Agreeableness also become stronger and achieve statistical significance. In a second model the mediating effect of personal traits becomes apparent, showing that the effect of Facebook usage loses statistical significance, the variable Emotional Stability becomes stronger, as does the statistically significant effect of Extraversion the statistical effect of Agreeableness turns to be negative. The explained variance in model 1 and 2 was 0.17 and 0.20, respectively.

We further tested the moderating effect of the entrepreneur's personality traits on the relationship between social media usage and business performance, multiplying the personality variables with the variables Twitter and Facebook and resulting in interaction terms for each. Statistical significance was achieved for the interaction term Agreeableness and Facebook on a negative sign (with a variance of 5%) and the interaction term Openness and Facebook on a positive sign (with a variance of 16%).

In conclusion, we show that some personality traits of entrepreneurs, (i.e. Emotional Stability and Extraversion), have impact on entrepreneurial performance. Further, we identify positive direct effects of social media usage on business performance. Lastly, we come to the conclusion that personal traits also mediate the relationship between social media usage and Entrepreneurial Performance, and partly confirm the mediating effects of the personality traits Openness and Agreeableness.

Bibliography

Aldrich, H., Zimmer, C. (1986). Entrepreneurship Through Social Networks. Ballinger Publishing Company, Cambridge, USA, 1986.

Alexa Inc. (2010). Traffic details from Alexa, Retrieved on February 20, 2011, from http://www.alexa.com/siteinfo/twitter.com

Alexa Inc. (2011). Traffic details from Alexa, Retrieved on February 20, 2011, from http://www.alexa.com/siteinfo/facebook.com

Allport, G. W., Odbert, H. S. (1936). Trait Names: A Psycho-Lexical Study. In: Psychological Monographs, Vol. 47, p211.

Almus, M., Nerlinger, E.A. (1999). Growth of New Technology-Based Firms: Which Factors Matter? Small Business Economics, 13(2):141154, 1999.

Alston, D. (2009). Article on: Social Media ROI - What's the 'Return on Ignoring'? Marketing Profs. Retrieved December 12, 2010, from https://www .marketingprofs.com/

Amichai-Hamburger, Y. et al. (2002). "On the Internet No One Knows I'm an Introvert": Extraversion, Neuroticism, and Internet Interaction. In: Cyberpsychology & Behavior, Vol. 5, Issue 2, p125-128.

Amit, R. et al. (1990). Entrepreneurial Ability, Venture Investments and Risk Sharing. Management Science, 36:12321245, 1990.

Amit, R. et al. (1998). Why Do Venture Capital Firms Exist? Theory and Canadian Evidence. Journal of Business Venturing, 13:441466, 1998.

Amit, R. et al. (2002). Journal of Economics & Management Strategy, 11(3):423452, 2002.

Baer, M. et al. (2008). The Personality Composition of Teams and Creativity: The Moderating Role of Team Creative Confidence. In: Journal of Creative Behavior, Vol. 42, Issue 4, p255-282.

Baron, R.M., Kenny, D.A (1986). The Moderator-Mediator Variable Distinction in Social Psychological Research: Conceptual, Strategic and Statistical Considerations. Journal of Personality Psychology 1986; 51:1173-1182.

Barrick, M. R. et al. (2001). Personality and Performance at the Beginning of the New Millennium: What Do We Know and Where Do We Go Next? In: International Journal of Selection and Assessment, Vol. 9, p9-30.

Barrick, M. R.; Mount, M. K. (1991). The Big Five Personality Dimensions and Job Performance: A Meta-Analysis. In: Personnel Psychology, Vol. 44, p1-26.

Baum, J. R.; Frese, M.; Baron, R. A. (Edt.) (2007). The Psychology of Entrepreneurship. Mahwah, NJ: Erlbaum (The organizational frontiers series).

Baum, J.A.C. et al. (2000). Don't Do It Alone: Alliance Network Composition and Start-ups' Performance in Canadian Biotechnology. Strategic Management Journal, 21:267294, 2000.

Baum, J.A.C., Silverman, B.S. (2004). Picking Winners or Building Them? Alliance, Intellectual, and Human Capital As Selection Criteria in Venture Financing and Performance of Biotechnology Start-ups. Journal of Business Venturing, 19:411 436, 2004.

Bergemann, D., Heger, U. (1998). Venture Capital Financing, Moral Hazard, and Learning. Journal of Banking & Finance, 22:703735, 1998.

Bialik, C. (2005). Measuring the Impact of Blogs Requires More Than Counting. In: The Wall Street Journal. Retrieved August 29, 2011, from http://online.wsj.com/public/article/0,,SB111685593903640572,00.html.

Bias, R. G. et al. (2010). An Exploratory Study of Visual and Psychological Correlates of Preference for Onscreen Subpixel-Rendered Text. In: Journal of the American Society for Information Science and Technology, Vol. 61, Issue 4, p745-757.

Birley, S. (1985). Role of Networks in the Entrepreneurial Process. Journal of Business Venturing, 1(1):107117, 1985.

Blechner, N. (2011). ARD news article on social media: The New Regular's Table. Retrieved February 10, 2011, from http://boerse.ard.de/content.jsp?key=dokument_505616

Block, J. (1995). A Contrarian View of the Five-Factor Approach to Personality Description. In: Psychological Bulletin, Vol. 117, p187-215.

Bolton Report (1971). Report of the Committee of Inquiry on Small Firms, chaired by J.E. Bolton, Cmnd. 4811, HMSO, London.

Bonacich, P. (1972). Factoring and Weighting Approaches to Clique Identification. Journal of Mathematical Sociology, 2 (1972), 113-120.

Bonacich, P. (1987). Power and Centrality: A Family of Measures. American Journal of Sociology 92 (1987), 1170-1182.

Borgatti,S.P. et al. (2002). Ucinet for Windows: Software for Social Network Analysis. Harvard, USA, 2007.

Bouwmeester, S. et al. (2004). Latent Class Regression Analysis for Describing Cognitive Developmental Phenomena: An Application to Transitive Reasoning. European Journal of Developmental Psychology, 1, 67-86.

Brandstätter, H. (1997). Becoming an Antrepreneur - A Question of Personality Structure? In: Journal of Economic Psychology, Vol. 18, p157-177.

Briegleb, V. (2010). Article on: Medienexperte: Zeitungen werden verschwinden, Retrieved January 20, 2011, from http://www.heise.de/newsticker/meldung/Medienexperte-Zeitungen-werden-verschwinden-908468.html

Brockhaus, R. H. et al. (1986). The Psychology of the Entrepreneur. In: Sexton, D. L.; Smilor, R. W. (Edt.): The Art and science of entrepreneurship. Cambridge, Mass.: Ballinger .

Brush, C.G., Vanderwerf, P.A. (1993). A Comparison of Methods and Sources for Obtaining Estimates of New Venture Performance. Journal of Business Venturing, 7, 157-170.

Burt, R.S. (1992). Structural Holes. Harvard University Press, Cambridge, MA.

Butt, S., Phillips, J. G. (2008). Personality and Self-Reported Mobile Phone Use. In: Computers in Human Behavior, Vol. 24, Issue 2, p346-360.

Bygrave, W.D. (1987). Syndicated Investments by Venture Capital Firms: A Networking Perspective. Journal of Business Venturing, 2:139154, 1987.

Bygrave, W.D. (1988). The Structure of the Investment Networks of Venture Capital Firms. Journal of Business Venturing, 3:137157, 1988.

Cable, D. M., Shane, S. (1997). A Prisoner's Dilemma Approach to Entrepreneur-Venture Capitalist Relationships. In: Academy of Management Review, Vol. 22, p142-176.

Carlson, N. (2011). Article on: Facebook Has More Than 600 Million Users, Goldman Tells Clients, Retrieved on February 20, 2011, from http://www.businessinsider.com/facebook-has-more-than-600-million-users-goldman-tells-clients-2011-1

Chandler, G.N., Hanks, S.H. (1993). Measuring the Performance of Emerging Businesses: A Validation Study. Journal of Business Venturing, 8, 391-408.

Ciavarella, M. A. et al. (2004). The Big Five and Venture Survival: Is There a Linkage? In: Journal of Business Venturing, Vol. 19, p465-483.

Coleman, J.S. (1988). Social Capital in the Creation of Human Capital. American Journal of Sociology, 94: 95-120.

Coleman, J.S. (1990). Foundations of Social Theory. Harvard University Press, Cambridge, MA.

Cooper, R. G. (1981). An Empirically Derived New Product Project Selection Model. In: Transactions on Engineering Management, Vol. 28, p54-61.

Corey, L. G. (1971). People Who Claim to Be Opinion Leaders: Identifying Their Characteristics by Self-Report. In: Journal of Marketing, Vol. 34, Issue 4, p48-53.

Correa, T. et al. (2010). Who Interacts on the Web?: The Intersection of Users' Personality and Social Media Use. In: Computers and Human Behavior, Vol. 26, p247-253.

Costa, P. T., McCrae, R. R. (1992). Revised NEO Personality Inventory (NEO-PI-R) and NEO Five Factor Inventory (NEO FFI) Professional Manual. Odessa: Psychological Assessment Resources.

Costello, K., Hodson, G. (2010). Exploring the Roots of Dehumanization: The role of Animal-Human Similarity in Promoting Immigrant Humanization. In: Group Processes & Intergroup Relations, Vol. 13, Issue 1, p3-22.

Cowling, D. (2010). Article on: Social Media Stats in Austrialia - Facebook Blogger, Myspace. Retrieved February 3, 2010, from http://www.socialmedianews.com.au/social-media-stats-in-australia-facebook-blogger-myspace/

Craig, S., Sorkin A. (2011). Goldman Offering Clients a Chance to Invest in Facebook. Retrieved August 29, 2011, from http://dealbook.nytimes.com/2011/01/02/goldman-invests-in-facebook-at-50-billion-valuation/.

Davis, T.J., Stetson, C.P. (1984). Creating Successful Venture-Backed Companies. Journal of Business Strategy 5:45-58.

Day, J. et al. (1998). Relationship Marketing: Its Key Role in Entrepreneurs' Long Range Planning, Vol. 31, No. 6, pp.828 - 837.

Debruyn, S. (2009). Article on: Measuring the Return-on-Investment of Social Media Campaigns. Retrieved February 25, 2011, from http://www.stephendebruyn.com/socialmedia/2009/12/28/measuring-the-roi-of-social-media-campaigns.html

DeCarolis, D. et al. (1999). Dynamic Capabilities and New Product Development in High Technology Ventures: An Empirical Analysis of New Biotechnology Firms. Journal of Business Venturing, 15:211229, 1999.

DeClercq, D. et al. (2008). Firm and Group Influences on Venture Capital Firms Involvement in New Ventures. Journal of Management Studies, 45(7):11691194, 2008.

DeClercq, D., Dimov, D. (2004). Explaining Venture Capital Firms Syndication Behavior: A Longitudinal Study. Venture Capital: An International Journal of Entrepreneurial Finance, 6(4):243256, 2004.

Dimov, D., Milanov, H. (2009). The Interplay of Need and Opportunity in Venture Capital Investment Syndication. Journal of Business Venturing, page forthcoming, 2009.

Dorsey, T. (1979). Operating Guidelines for Effective Venture Capital Funds Management. #3 in a technical series. Austin, TX: University of Texas.

Ebner, W. et al. (2005). Blogofy or Die, in: PR Magazin, Issue 2005, Nb. 12.

Eisenegger, M. (2005). Reputation in der Mediengesellschaft. Konstitution - Issues Monitoring - Issues Management, VS Verlag für Sozialwissenschaften, Wiesbaden.

Facebook Inc. (2011). Facebook Factsheets, Retrieved February 26, 2011, from http://www.facebook.com/press/info.php?factsheet

Ferris, G. R. et al. (2009). Interaction of Job-Limiting Pain and Political Skill on Job Satisfaction and Organizational Citizenship Behavior. In: Journal of Managerial Psychology, Vol. 24, Issue 7-8, p584-608.

Fraser, K. (2008), Article on: The Evolving Nature Of Technology Adoption. Retrieved on March 10, 2011, from http://Weblog.getglue.com/?p=1090

Fried, V.H., Hisrich, R.D., (1995). The Venture Capitalist: A Relationship Investor. Calif. Management Review. 37 (2), 101-114.

Furnham, A. et al. (2009). Personality, Motivation and Job Satisfaction: Hertzberg Meets the Big Five. In: Journal of Managerial Psychology, Vol. 24, Issue 7-8, p765-779.

Gaffney, A., Ferrante, A. (2010). A DemandGen Report, Whitepaper: Breaking Out of the Funnel: A Look Inside the Mind of the New B2B Buyer.

Gartner, W. B. (1988). "Who Is an entrepreneur?" Is the Wrong Guestion. In: Entrepreneurship Theory and Practice, Vol. 13, Iusse 4, p47-68.

Gellatly, I. R. (1996). Conscientiousness and Job Performance: Test of a Cognitive Process Model. In: Journal of Applied Psychology, Vol. 81, p474-482.

Geuens, M. et al. (2009). A New Measure of Brand Personality. In: International Journal of Research in Marketing, Vol. 26, Issue 2, p97-107.

Gill, K. (2004). How Can We Measure the Influence of the Blogosphere? Conference 2004. New York. Organisator: WWW2004 Conference. Retrieved August 29, 2011, from http://faculty.washington.edu/kegill/pub/www2004_blogosphere_gill.pdf.

Gompers, P.A, Lerner, L. (2001). The Venture Capital Revolution. The Journal of Economic Perspectives, 15(2):145168, 2001.

Gompers, P.A. (1995). Optimal Investment, Monitoring, and the Staging of Venture Capital. The Journal of Finance, 50:14611489, 1995.

Gorman, M., Sahlman, W.A., (1989). What Do Venture Capitalists Do? Journal of Business Venturing 4, 231-248.

Gosling, S. D. et al. (2003). A Very Brief Measure of the Big-Five Personality Domains. In: Journal of Research in Personality, Vol. 37, p504-528.

Granovetter, M. (1973). The Strength of Weak Ties. The American journal of sociology, 1973.

Granovetter, M. (1983). The Strength of Weak Ties: A Network Theory Revisited. Sociological theory, 1983.

Granovetter, M. (1985). Economic Action and Social Structure: The Problem of Embeddedness. American Journal of Sociology, 91(3):481510, Nov. 1985.

Grant, A. M., Ashford, S. J. (2008). The Dynamics of Proactivity at Work. In: Research in Organizational Behavior, Vol. 28, p3-34.

Graziano, W. G., Eisenberg, N. (1997). Agreeableness; A Dimension of Personality. In: Hogan, Robert (Edt.): Handbook of Personality Psychology. San Diego: Academic Press .

Greve, A., Sala, J.W. (2003). Social Network and Entrepreneurship. Entrepreneurship, Theory & Practice, 28(1):122, 2003.

Gruber, M. (2005). Marketingplanung von Unternehmensgründungen - Eine Theoretische und Empirische Analyse, Deutscher Universitaets Verlag, Wiesbaden.

Hansen, E.L. (1995). Entrepreneurial Networks and New Organization Growth. Entrepreneurship: Theory and Practice, 19:719, 1995.

Harris, A (2009). Article on: Contractors Market With Social Media. Air Conditioning, Heating & Refrigeration News from December 21, 2009. Retrieved February 25, 2011 from Research Library, ProQuest.

Hauswiesner, F. (2006). Venture Capital USA. Working paper.

Hellmann, T. (1998). The Allocation of Control Rights in Venture Capital Contracts. The RAND Journal of Economics, 29(1):5776, 1998.

Hellmann, T., Puri, M. (2002). Venture Capital and the Professionalization of Start-Up Firms: Empirical Evidence. The Journal of Finance, 57(1):169198, 2002.

Heneman, H. G. (1974). Comparisons of Self- and Superior Ratings of Managerial Performance. In: Journal of Applied Psychology, Vol. 59, Issue 5, p638-642.

Hills, G. et al. (2010). History, Theory and Evidence of Entrepreneurial Marketing - An Overview, International Journal of Entrepreneurship and Innovation Management, Vol. 11, No. 1.

Hoffmann, D. (2010). Article on: Social Media Nutzerzahlen und Trends in Deutschland 1/2010. Retrieved February 10, 2011, from http://www.socialmedia-Weblog.de/2010/04/social-media-nutzerzahlen-und-trends-in-deutschland/

Hogan, Robert (Edt.) (1997). Handbook of Personality Psychology. San Diego: Academic Press.

Hong, S., Yang, S.-U. (2009). Effects of Reputation, Relational Satisfaction, and Customer-Company Identification on Positive Word-of-Mouth Intensions, Journal of Public Relations Research, 21 (4). p.381-403.

Hopp, C., Rieder, F. (2010). What Drives Venture Capital Syndication? Applied Economics. Forthcoming

Horizont Study (2009). 60 Prozent der deutschen Unternehmen nutzen Social Media. Retrieved December 15, 2009, from http://www.horizont.net/aktuell/digital/pages/protected/Studie-60-Prozent-der-deutschen-Unternehmen-nutzen-Social-Media_88992.html

Hoyt, C. L. et al. (2009). Choosing the Best (Wo)man for the Job: The Effects of Mortality Salience, Sex, and Gender Stereotypes on Leader Evaluations. In: Leadership Quarterly, Vol. 20, Issue 2, p233-246.

Huesing, A.(2010). Article on: Facebook saugt die Konkurrenz auf - Stayfriends im freien Fall - Soziale Netzwerke im AGOF-Check. Retrieved February 15, 2010, from http://www.deutsche-startups.de/2010/12/16/facebook-saugt-die-konkurrenz-auf-stayfriends-im-freien-fall-soziale-netzwerke-im-agof-check/

Huffaker, D., Calvert, S. (2005). Gender, Identity and Language Use in Teenage Blogs. In: Journal of Computer-Mediated Communication, Vol. 10, Issue 2. Retrieved August 29, 2011, from http://jcmc.indiana.edu/vol10/issue2/huffaker.html.

IfD Allensbach (2010). Study retrieved February 10, 2011, from http://de.statista.com/statistik/diagramm/studie/22662/umfrage/betreiben-eines-eigenen-web-blogs-(online-tagebuch)

Ivcevic, Z., Mayer, J. (2009). Mapping Dimensions of Creativity in the Life-Space. In: Creativity Research Journal, Vol. 21, Issue 2-3, p152-165.

Jack, S.L. et al. (2005). The Role of Family Members in Entrepreneurial Networks: Beyond the Boundaries of the Family Rm. Family Business Review, 18(2):135154, 2005.

John, O. P., Srivastava, S. (1999). The Big Five Trait Taxonomy: History, Measurement, and Theoretical Perspectives. In: L. A. Pervin; John, O. P. (Edt.): Handbook of Personality: Theory and Research. 2. ed., 3. [print]. New York NY u.a.: Guilford Press, p102-138.

Judge, T. A. et al. (2002). Personality and Leadership: A Qualitative and Quantitative Review. In: Journal of Applied Psychology, Vol. 87, p765-780.

Kaplan, A. M., Haenlein, M. (2010). Users of the World, Unite! The Challenges and Opportunities of Social Media. In: Business Horizons, Vol. 53, p59-68.

Keasey, K. and Watson, R. (1991). The State of the Art of Small Firm Failure Prediction: Achievements and Prognosis, International Small Business Journal, Vol. 9 No. 4, p11-28.

Kelly, N. (2010). Article on: 4 Ways to Measure Social Media and Its Impact on Your Brand. Retrieved January 2, 2011, from http://www.socialmediaexaminer.com/4-ways-measure-social-media-and-its-impact-on-your-brand

Kiellisch, T. (2009), Article on: Die wichtigsten Trends für 2010. Retrieved March 12, 2011, from: http://www.business-wissen.de/marketing/online-marketing-die-wichtigsten-trends-fuer-2010/

Kratzer, J., Lettl, C. (2009). Distinctive Roles of Lead Users and Opinion Leaders in the Social Networks of Schoolchildren. In: Journal of Consumer Research, Vol. 36, p646-659.

L. A. Pervin, John, O. P. (Edt.) (1999). Handbook of Personality: Theory and Research. 2. ed., 3. [print]. New York NY u.a.: Guilford Press.

Landers, R., Lounsbury, J. W. (2006). An Investigation of Big Five and Narrow Personality Traits in Relation to Internet Usage. In: Computers and Human Behavior, Vol. 22, p283-293.

Larson, A. (1991). Partner networks: Leveraging External Ties to Improve Entrepreneurial Performance. Journal of Business Venturing, 6:173188, 1991.

Larson, A. (1992). Network Dyads in Entrepreneurial Settings: A Study of the Governance of Exchange Relationships. Administrative Science Quarterly, 37(1):76 104, 1992.

Lechner, C., Dowling, M. (2003). Firm Networks: External Relationships As Sources for the Growth and Competitiveness of Entrepreneurial Rms. Entrepreneurship & Regional Development, 15:126, 2003.

Lee, D. Y., Tsang, E. W. K. (2001). The Effects of Entrepreneurial Personality, Background and Network Activities on Venture Growth. In: Journal of Management Studies, Vol. 38, Issue 4, p583-602.

Lerner, J. (1994). The Syndication of Venture Capital Investments. Financial Management, 23:1627, 1994.

Li, J., Chignell, M. (2010). Birds of a Feather: How Personality Influences Weblog Writing and Reading. In: International Journal of Human-Computer Studies, Vol. 68, Issue 9, p589-602.

Littunen, H. (2000). Networks and Local Environmental Characteristics in the Survival of New Firms. Small Business Economics, 15(1):5971, 2000.

Ljungqvist, A. et al. (2007). Whom You Know Matters: Venture Capital Networks and Investment Performance. The Journal of Finance, 62(1):251302, 2007.

Ljungqvist, A. et al. (2010). Networking as a Barrier to Entry and the Competitive Supply of Venture Capital. The Journal of Finance, 65(3):829859, 2010.

Locke, E. A. et al. (1988). The Determinants of Goal Commitment. In: Academy of Management Review, Vol. 13, Issue 1, p23-39.

Lockett, A., Wright, M. (1999). The Syndication of Venture Capital Investments. Omega, 29:175190, 1999.

Lua, J.W., Beamishb, P.W. (2006). Partnering Strategies and Performance of SMEs' International Joint Ventures. Journal of Business Venturing, Volume 21, Issue 4, July 2006, Pages 461-486.

Mai, J. (2009). Article on: Corporate-Twitter-Studie - So twittern deutsche Unternehmen. Retrieved February 20, 2011, from http://karrierebibel.de/corporate-twitter-studie-so-twittern-deutsche-unternehmen

Mangold, W. G., Faulds, D. J. (2009). Social Media: The New Hybrid Element of the Promotion Mix. In: Business Horizons, Vol. 52, p357-365.

Manigart, S. et al. (2006). Venture Capitalists' Decision to Syndicate. Entrepreneurship Theory & Practice, 30:131153, 2006.

Markman, G. D., Baron, R. A. (2003). Person-Entrepreneurship Fit: Why Some People Are More Successful As Entrepreneurs Than Others. In: Human Resource Management Review, Vol. 13, p281-301.

Martin, L.L. et al. (1990). Assimilation and Contrast As a Function of People's Willingness and Ability to Expend Effort in Forming an Impression. Journal of Personality and Social Psychology, Vol 59(1), Jul 1990, 27-37

Matthews, G. et al. (2008). Personality Traits. 2. ed., 4. print. Cambridge: Cambridge Univ.

Press.

Matyka, D. (2011). University paper. Social Media - Temporary Trend or Sustainable Revolution?

Mauro, C. (2009). Article on: What US Airways Flight 1549's Ditching in the Hudson River Teaches Companies About How to Create World-Class User Interface Design Solutions. Retrieved February 10, 2011, from http://www.mauronewmedia.com/Weblog/2009/04/what-us-airways-flight-1549s-ditching-in-the-hudson-river-teaches-companies-about-how-to-create-world-class-user-interface-design-solutions/

Mayer-Uellner, R. (2003). Das Schweigen der Lurker. Politische Partizipation und soziale Kontrolle in Online-Diskussionsforen. München: Fischer(Reinhard).

McCrae, R. R. (1987). Creativity, Divergent Thinking, and Openness to Experience. In: Journal of Personality and Social Psychology, Vol. 52, p1258-1265.

McCrae, R. R., Costa, P. T., JR (1999). A Five-Factor Theory of Personality. In: L. A. Pervin; John, O. P. (Edt.): Handbook of Personality: Theory and Research. 2. ed., 3. [print]. New York NY: Guilford Press, p139-153.

McDougall, P.P. et al. (1992). Modeling New Venture Performance: An Analysis of New Venture Strategy, Industry Structure and Venture Origin. Journal of Business Venturing, 7, 267-289.

McFadden, D. (1987). Regression-Based Specification Tests For the Multinomial Logit Model. Journal of Econometrics, 34 (1-2), 63-82.

McGann, R. (2004). The Blogosphere By the Numbers. Retrieved August 29, 2011, from www.clickz.com/stats/sectors/traffic_patterns/article.php/3438891.

Miller, C., Sheperd, D. (2004). Blogging As Social Action: A Genre Analysis of the Weblog. Retrieved August 29, 2011, from http://Weblog.lib.umn.edu/blogosphere/blogging_as_social_action_a_genre_analysis_of_th e_Weblog.html.

Moeller, E. (2005). Die heimliche Medienrevolution. Wie Weblogs, Wikis und freie Software die Welt verändern. 1. edition, Hannover: Heise (Telepolis Magazin der Netzkultur).

Möller, E. (2005). Die heimliche Medienrevolution. Wie Weblogs, Wikis und freie Software die Welt verändern, Heise, Hannover.

Mooradian, T. et al. (2006). Who trusts? Personality, Trust and Knowledge Sharing. In: Management Learning, Vol. 37, Issue 4, p523-540.

Morrison, K. A. (1997). How Franchise Job Satisfaction and Personality Affects Performance, Organizational Commitment, Franchisor Relations, and Intention to Remain. In: Journal of Small Business Management, Vol. 35, Issue 3, p39-76.

Motowidlo, S. J., Peterson, N. G. (2008). Effects of Organizational Perspective on Implicit Trait Policies About Correctional Officers' Job Performance. In: Human Performance, Vol. 21, Issue 4, p396-413.

Murphy, G. (1996). Measuring Performance in Entrepreneurship Research, Journal of Business Research, Vol. 36, 1996, p15-23.

Murphy, G. (1996). Measuring Performance in Entrepreneurship Research. In: Journal of Business Research, Vol. 36, p15-23.

Neuberger, C. (2005). Weblogs verstehen. Über den Strukturwandel der Öffentlichkeit im Internet, in Picot, A., Fischer, T. (eds): Weblogs professionell. Grundlagen, Konzepte und Praxis im unternehmerischen Umfeld, Hannover, p113-129.

Nicholson, N. et al. (2005). Personality and Domain-Specific Risktaking. In: Journal of Risk Research, Vol. 8, p157-176.

Nielson Report (2011). Article on: Social Networks/Blogs Now Account for One in Every Four and a Half Minutes Online. Retrieved January 9, 2011, from http://Weblog.nielsen.com/nielsenwire/global/social-media-accounts-for-22-percent-of-time-online/

Oreilly, T. (2004). What is Web 2.0. Conference Presentation.

Oreilly, T. (2007). What is Web 2.0: Design Patterns and Business Models for the Next Generation of Software. In: International Journal of Digital Economics, Vol. 65, p17-37.

Pfeiffer, T. (2010). Article on: Anzahl der Twitteraccounts in Deutschland, Österreich und der Schweiz (und Liechtenstein:-). Retrieved Frebruary 26, 2011, from http://webevangelisten.de/anzahl-twitteraccounts-deutschland-oesterreich-schweiz/

Podolny, J.M., Page, K.L. (1998). Network Forms of Organization. Annual Review of Sociology, 24: 57-76.

Poropat, A. E.; Jones, L. (2009). Development and Validation of a Unifactorial Measure of Citizenship Performance. In: Journal of Occupational and Organizational Psychology, Vol. 82, Issue 4, p851-869.

Powell, W.W. (1990). Neither Market nor Hierarchy: Network Forms of Organization. Research in Organizational Behaviour, 12:295336, 1990.

Prebluda, A. (2010). Article on: We're number two! Facebook Moves Up One Big Spot in the Charts. Retrieved December 15, 2010, from http://Weblog.compete.com/2010/02/17/we%E2%80%99re-number-two-facebook-moves-up-one-big-spot-in-the-charts/

Prescott, L. (2010). Article on: 54% of US Internet Users on Facebook, 27% on MySpace. Retrieved January 9, 2011, from http://digital.venturebeat.com/2010/02/10/54-of-us-internet-users-on-facebook-27-on-myspace/trackback/

Quantcast Audience Profile (2010). Twitter Growth. Retrieved on February 20, 2011, from http://www.quantcast.com/twitter.com

Rain, K. (2009). Twitter Study Reveals Interesting Results About Usage. San Antonio, Texas: Pear. Analytics. Retrieved on December 15, 2010 from http://www.pearanalytics.com/Weblog/wp-content/uploads/2010/05/Twitter-Study-August-2009.pdf

Rauch, A., Frese, M. (2007): Born to Be an Entrepreneur? Revisiting the Personality Approach to Entrepreneurship. In: Baum, J. R.; Frese, M.; Baron, R. A. (Edt.): The Psychology of Entrepreneurship. Mahwah, NJ: Erlbaum (The organizational frontiers series), p41-65.

Rentfrow, P. J. et al. (2009). You Are What You Listen To: Young People's Stereotypes About Music Fans. In: Group Processes & Intergroup Relations, Vol. 12, Issue 3, p329-344.

Richards, R. (2006). Online Marketing Success Stories, Atlantic Publishing Group, Ocala, Florida.

Ross, C. et al. (2009). Personality and Motivations Associated With Facebook Use. In:

Computers in Human Behavior, Vol. 25,p578-586.

Rossmann, A. (2010). Web 2.0 Perspektiven für die Marketing & Corporate Communication. Retrieved August 29, 2011, from http://www.competence-site.de/downloads/c4/a9/i_file_276197/web_2.0_perspektiven_fuer_die_marketing_and_corporate_communication.pdf.

Schmidt, J. (2006). Weblogs - eine kommunikationssoziologische Studie, UVK Verlagsgesellschaft, Konstanz.

Schulte, R. (2010). Entrepreneurial Marketing and the Role of Information - Evidence From Young Service Ventures, International Journal of Entrepreneurship and Innovation Management, Vol. 11, No. 1.

Schumpeter, J. (1942). From Capitalism, Socialism and Democracy. Harper, New York, USA, 1942.

Schumpeter, J. A. (1939). BUSINESS CYCLES. A Theoretical, Historical and Statistical Analysis of the Capitalist Process. New York.

Sexton, D. L., Smilor, R. W. (Edt.) (1986). The Art and Science of Entrepreneurship. Cambridge, Mass.: Ballinger.

Shane, S., Cable, D. (2002). Network Ties, Reputation, and the Financing of New Ventures. Management Science, 48(3):364381, 2002.

Smith, D. (2009). Financial Bootstrapping and Social Capital: How Technology-Based Start-Ups Fund Innovation, International Journal Entrepreneurship and Innovation Management, Vol. 10, No. 2, 2009.

Smith, T. (2009). The Social Media Revolution, International Journal of Market Research, Vol. 51, Issue 4.

Sorenson, O., Stuart, T.E. (2001). Syndicating Networks and the Spatial Distribution of Venture Capital Investments. American Journal of Sociology, 106(6):1546 1588, 2001.

Sorenson, O., Stuart, T.E. (2008). Bringing the Context Back In: Settings and the Search for Syndicate Partners in Venture Capital Investment Networks. Administrative Science Quarterly, 53 (2008): 266-294

Stewart, W. H., Roth, P. L. (2001). Risk Propensity Differences Between Entrepreneurs and

Managers: A Metaanalytic Review. In: Journal of Applied Psychology, Vol. 86, Issue 1, p145-153.

Stuart, T.E. et al. (1999). Interorganizational Indorsement and the Performance of Entrepreneurial Ventures. Administrative Science Quarterly, 44: 315-349.

Taxali G. (2009). Article on: Cashing on Tweets. Computerworld Magazine from September 21, 2008, p24.

Tsai, W., Ghoshal, S., (1998). Social Capital and Value Creation: The Role of Intrafirm Networks. Academy of Management Journal, 41: 464-476.

Twitter Inc. (2009). Article on: There Is a List for That. Retrieved on January 15, 2011 from http://Weblog.twitter.com/2009/10/theres-list-for-that.html

van de Garde-Perik, E. et al. (2008). Investigating Privacy Attitudes and Behavior in Relation to Personalization. In: Social Science Computer Review, Vol. 26, Issue 1, p20-43.

Vermunt, J.K, Magidson, J. (2003). Latent Class Models for Classification. Computational Statistics and Data Analysis, 41,3-4, 531-537.

Vermunt, J.K. (2003). Applications of Latent Class Analysis in Social Science Research. Lecture Notes in Artificial Intelligence, 2711, 22-36.

Wassermann, S., Faust, K. (1994). Social Network Analysis: Methods and Applications. Cambridge University Press, Cambridge, UK, 1994.

Watson, J. (2007). Modeling the Relationship Between Networking and Firm Performance. Journal of Business Venturing, 22:852874, 2007.

Watson, K. et al. (1995). Small Business Start-Ups: Success Factors and Support Implications, International Journal of Entrepreneurial Behaviour & Research, Bradford & Leeds, UK.

Wright, M., Lockett, A. (2003). The Structure and Management of Alliances: Syndication in the Venture Capital Industry. Journal of Management Studies, 40(8):20732102, 2003.

Xia, L. et al. (2009). Exploring Negative Group Dynamics Adversarial Network, Personality, and Performance in Project Groups. In: Management Communication Quarterly, Vol. 23, Issue 1, p32-62.

Zerfaß, A., Boelter, D. (2005). Die neuen Meinungsmacher - Weblogs als Herausforderung für Kampagnen, Marketing, PR und Medien, Nausner & Nausner, Graz.

Zhao, H. et al. (2010). The Relationship of Personality to Entrepreneurial Intentions and Performance: A Meta-Analytic Review. In: Journal of Management, Vol. 36, Issue 2, p381-404.

Zhao, H., Seibert, S. E. (2006). The Big Five Personality Dimensions and Entrepreneurial Status: A Meta-Analytical Review. In: Journal of Applied Psychology, Vol. 91, Issue 2, p259-271.

Zucker, L. et al. (1996). Social Networks, Learning, and Flexibility: Sourcing Scientic Knowledge in New Biotechnology Firms. Organization Science, 7(4):428443, 1996.

2 Analysis of perceived importance, objective usage patterns and efficiency of social media activities among German Internet and technology start-up companies

Author: Matyka, D.

Abstract

Micro-blogging sites like Twitter and social network sites such as Facebook and Weblogs have grown rapidly in recent years, allowing customers to actively participate in the communication process, sharing customer opinions and providing marketers a tool to reach almost everyone anywhere and anytime, at almost no cost. This research focuses on evaluating social media usage and efficiency patterns of early adaptors, in particular among German Internet and technology start-ups founded between 2004 and 2009. In this paper the author investigates the subjective importance of Twitter, Facebook, and corporate Weblogs with distinction to strategic and marketing objectives. Moreover, the author compares these subjective assumptions regarding their importance by conducting research on objective usage patterns of these social media platforms. The author develops a financial performance indicator applicable to start-ups and correlates this parameter to the actual usage of social media.

2.1 Introduction

Social media was one of the major trends in communication in 2009 and 2010 (Kiellisch, 2009), and will develop into a mass-market communication phenomenon in 2011 as numerous different actors already participate in this communication area. The victorious spread of Facebook and Twitter during the last 12 months has made social media a widely discussed topic. Communication paradigms have being changed structurally and traditional media starts to rely more and more on social media as a primary source of information gathering.

The possibility of direct and free-of-charge communication with stakeholders facilitates an increasing attractiveness among all kinds of companies. Meanwhile, approximately half of the German DAX50-listed companies rely on platforms such as Facebook and more than 70% on Twitter as their social media marketing platform (Blechner 2011); having said that, it is not trivial to measure the efficiency of social media. Social media experts strive to calculate the return-on-investment, but a rather rudimentary base of knowledge hinders them in holistically evaluating the importance of social media platforms. The number of companies actively participating within social media grows at rapid velocity; the evaluation of its associated chances and risks determines the importance of this paper. The fear of losing control over the customer-communication process, the uncertainty about its potential, and the return-on-investment argument are areas of particular interest among social media experts and researchers.

Nevertheless, while social media usually embraces all kinds of different platforms and applications for the exchange of user-generated content, this study focuses on the micro-blogging service Twitter, the social networking site Facebook, and corporate Weblogs as the most widely used Internet-based company communication channels. Social media, alongside almost all technological inventions of digital media, is mostly adapted early by technology start-up companies rather than brick-and-mortar corporations (Fraser, 2008). Entrepreneurship and marketing become „intersected" while „successful entrepreneurs practice marketing and the better marketers act entrepreneurial" (Day et al., 1998; Hills et al., 2010). This might be due to legal restrictions or uncertainty – corporations are oftentimes latecomers. The author therefore analyzes the usage of social media among technology start-up companies that use these kinds of media because of its cost and time neutrality, and in its early stages, oftentimes referred to as beta versions.

The present study tries to measure the success of social media from a return-on-investment perspective. In a first step, 258 German Internet and media start-up companies were asked through a web-based survey to rate the importance of social media (importance perception analysis). The paper aims to identify how important social media is for strategic and marketing objectives in general. In a second step, crawling and data mining algorithms were used to analyze the actual usage of different social media platforms. The study attempts to shed light on how start-ups use social media in practice (objective usage analysis). These outcomes were correlated to the before surveyed perceived importance. In a final step, the objective social media usage patterns were put in relation to certain success factors (efficiency analysis) to analyze if start-ups using social media are more successful than start-ups not using social media. The study aims to determine perception and efficiency of social media usage by verifying three propositions to find out if companies are merely following a widely established trend or if social media is directly correlated to (monetary) success, and therefore sustainably revolutionizing the way companies communicate with their stakeholders.

2.2 Literature review and theoretical background

2.2.1 Introduction to social media

The field of social media is relatively new and as of yet quite unexplored. It therefore provides numerous research opportunities. User-driven technologies such as the micro-blogging service Twitter and social networks such as Facebook or Weblogs have revolutionized the market over the last few years. Collectively, this trend in social communication, community formation, and user-generated content is uniformly tagged as social media, i.e. web-based technologies that turn communication into interactive dialogues (Kaplan & Haenlein, 2010). Mass media, previously controlled by professionals without supporting customer dialogue, is shifting to a public communication with the power of re-orientating the economy (Smith, 2009).

In addition to purely thematic application areas of research, sociological communication work focuses on network- and activity-centred research. The former deals with the dynamics and shape of social networks and the latter focuses on the social actions of individual actors as the main starting point for their investigations (Eisenegger, 2005).

2.2.2 Social media landscape

The public conversation is often led by social media as the first source of information gathering; recent examples include a plane ditching on the Hudson river in New York, where a passenger took the first photos and used social media to spread them, and mass media finally circulated them around the world (Mauro, 2009).

By March 2010, more the 30 million German Internet users were affiliated with a social community. Although the micro-blogging service Twitter currently holds just over 350,000 user accounts in Germany, it comprises a variety of opinion leaders and experts (Pfeiffer, 2010).

Social media empowers companies to directly interact with their target groups. Public relations, marketing, distribution, recruiting and employer branding, as well as the ability to include customers directly in product and service development all offer companies a wide range of new opportunities. Nevertheless, most companies, especially digital ones in early stages, only use social media to communicate and interact with their stakeholders, thus enlarging their attractiveness and popularity in a given market. Hence, word-of-mouth is a vital part of social media activities, as customer opinions and recommendations are generally more accepted in terms of authenticity compared to, for example, a company's press release (Hong & Yang, 2009).

The top three networks in Germany are *VZnetworks*, *wer-kennt-wen* and Facebook, with the last achieving the highest growth rates (Huesing, 2010). Facebook, after Google, is the most visited website in Germany, and one of seven communities or social media platforms among the top 20 visited websites. The *VZnetworks*, a group of social networking sites owned by publishing house *Holtzbrinck*, accumulated 16.6 million users with over 13 million open social applications installed, whereas Facebook accounts for nearly eighteen million users in Germany alone. Twitter represents one million German tweets—i.e. 140-character-long messages posted by users—per day. *Nielsonwire* measured online time spent to be four hours in social media per day (Hoffmann, 2010).

Taking a view on international figures of social media, recent statistics show that social networking sites account for 22% of all time spent online in the United States (Nielson, 2011) and a total of 234 million people age 13 or older in the

USA used mobile devices in December 2009 (Prescott, 2009) to connect to social network sites. Over 25% of U.S. page views occurred at one of the top social networking sites in December 2009 (Prescott, 2009), with Australia leading in the social media usage statistics, in terms of Facebook, ranking highest with nine hours a month from nine million users (Cowling, 2010).

2.2.3 Start-up companies as object of investigation

As this paper focuses solely on start-up companies, it is important to understand why the author believes start-ups to be the evident object of investigation. Many start-up companies fail to develop into successful new businesses after an infancy period (Watson and Scott, 1996). This is partly owed to the fact that innovative start-up companies "require access to a range of resources including capital" (Smith, 2009).

The success and failure determinants are manifold, and research oftentimes takes statistical models of financial characteristics from models of established companies to evaluate start-up performance (Keasey and Watson, 1991). While those models might be appropriate for the identification of success determinants regarding corporations, they clearly lack a dedicated focus on the characteristics of small ventures. Although it might be the founder that inherits an influencing and success-determinant role (Bolton Report, 1971), this investigation focuses on the impact of the application of the right social media strategy as an internal environmental factor of entrepreneurial behaviour.

Gray and Stanworth (1991) pointed out that success depends on a complex set of interrelated factors, and it becomes evident that this multi-dimensional phenomenon that influences the probability of running a success business becomes even more complex when the start-up grows. This paper focuses on start-up companies, as the author believes the set of probable success determinants is likely to be smaller when running a small start-up company rather than an established business.

Aside from financial resources, marketing is widely interpreted as a success factor for companies of all stages and sizes. Several authors point out that „entrepreneurial marketing should have a special impact on new ventures' success" (Gruber, 2005; Schulte, 2010). Further, Hills points out that business owners nowadays tend to be more customer-driven (2010) and social media clearly provides the means to act this way.

2.2.4 How to embrace return-on-investment in online marketing, especially social media

While start-ups engage in social media in all kinds of forms, brick-and-mortar companies do not. The missing means of evaluating quantitatively the financial success of social media hinders executives from installing wide social media programs (Harris, 2009). There are several ways that companies usually measure their success. Quantitative measurement indicators, for example, are key performance indicators that measure directly correlated success of social media to return-on-investment or revenues (Debruyn, 2009).

In order to measure the effectiveness (which platforms to use) and efficiency (how to use these platforms) of online marketing based on the value of click-through rates, conversion rates and other website tracking numbers are widely accepted and standardized in the online world (Richards, 2006).

The calculation of return-on-investment in this area is, therefore, well institutionalized. However, within the field of social media, marketers tend to measure activity rates, but oftentimes encounter barriers to measure their value, i.e. return-on-investment (Taxali, 2009). Barriers include a lack of dedicated resources to perform the measurement, a lack of knowledge of which variables to measure, and a general lack of applicable tools. Further investigation shows that as many as 20% of marketers say that social media is primarily not about return-on-investment (Alston, 2009).

Social media expert Nicole Kelly (2010) from *social media examiner* released a comprehensive article on the lead generation funnel, a category-driven approach of how to measure social media. The first category depicts the measurement of social media exposure and describes how many people a message could potentially reach.

Figure 2: Five categories of social media measurement

Retain	Funnel Category	Metrics
	Exposure	Visits, views, followers, fans, subscribers, brand mentions
	Influence	Share of voice, sentiment, top influencers report (Radian6)
	Engagement	Clicks, retweets, shares, @replies, DMs, wall posts, comments
	Action / Convert	Content downloads, webinar attendees, lead generation forms, pitches/proposals
Track repeat business and retention	$$	Online sales, phone sales, in-person sales

Source: Adapted from Kelly (2010)

The most important category describes measuring the *engagement*, such as clicks on social media links, but also quantitative Weblog engagement indicators such as comments. So-called retweets, i.e. the messages people send within Twitter that were re-sent by other people, or the pure amount of fans within Facebook, are purely quantitative key performance indicators that do not allow for any qualitative analysis. Therefore, within the category *influence*, qualitative indicators that refer to qualitative content such as the information value or professionalism of posts (within Weblogs) or tonality/sentiment of tweets (within Twitter) are mentioned as another possibility of return-on-investment measurement. All the aforementioned categories are more or less referring to the concept of brand awareness, as opposed to the category *action and convert*, which directly measures lead generation or sales and is oftentimes compared to traditional ROI-driven key performance indicators.

The above arguments led us to formulate three propositions that are empirically explored:

P1: Start-ups value social media platforms as being important for their strategic and marketing objectives.

P2: Start-ups are using social media in practice according to their perceived importance.

P3: Start-ups using social media are more successful in financial terms than start-ups not using social media.

2.3 Methodology

To address the first proposition, the author conducted a web-based online survey of 258 Internet and technology start-ups' founding management executives, asking for the general subjective importance of Facebook, Twitter, and corporate Weblogs with regard to the company's strategic and marketing objectives.

The second proposition was addressed by analyzing numerous usage patterns of social media. To this end, the author programmed multiple algorithms that crawled the diverse services for a period of 30 days. In a further step, the findings were correlated to the answers received in the survey.

To test the third proposition, the author also included several questions in the survey with regard to the financial status and financing of the sampled start-ups. The author asked for their financial status quo and the type of external financing received.

2.3.1 Research Design

Recent years have witnessed the rise of both Twitter as a social communication platform and Facebook as a social networking platform. Alongside corporate Weblogs, this new media currently belongs to the most popular new media tools. All of the three media can be seen as communication platforms allowing for user communication in a reciprocal way, acting as content creators and content consumers. Although the author studied usage patterns of video sites such as YouTube, Podcasting services and other media as well, it is believed – with regard to usage and platform growth – that those three platforms are the most important ones. Therefore, the author expects the results to be an objective measurement of the entire social media efficiency.

Twitter

The so-called micro-blogging service or mobile social network site Twitter launched in July 2006 and has since then reached an audience of almost 200,000,000 user profiles since its inception (Quantcast, 2010), ranking as the tenth most visited website worldwide by *Alexa*, a traffic measurement company (Alexa, 2010). The service allows users to post 140-character-long text-based messages or updates, well known as 'tweets,' to a network of people receiving those messages, known as 'followers.' Users can decide to subscribe to those text-based messages of other users; this is known as 'following' (Twitter, 2009).

A mutual permission to follow tweets is not necessary by default settings, but users can opt-in to hide their update communication from outside followers. Those tweets are sorted, analogously to a Weblog, in a chronological order, giving each user a dedicated destination site with a unique resource locator (short: URL).

Users can upload and receive tweets using multiple devices, among them the Twitter website, compatible external applications using the Twitter application programming interface (short: API), Instant Messaging or Short Message Services.

Kelly Rain (2009), together with research firm *Pear analytics,* conducted a study on Twitter, analyzing the content of more than 2,000 tweets during a two-week period. The results categorize Twitter content into six categories, including news, spam, self-promotion, pointless babble, conversational and pass along value:

Figure 3: Usage patterns of Twitter according to a study from Pear analytics (Content of tweets)

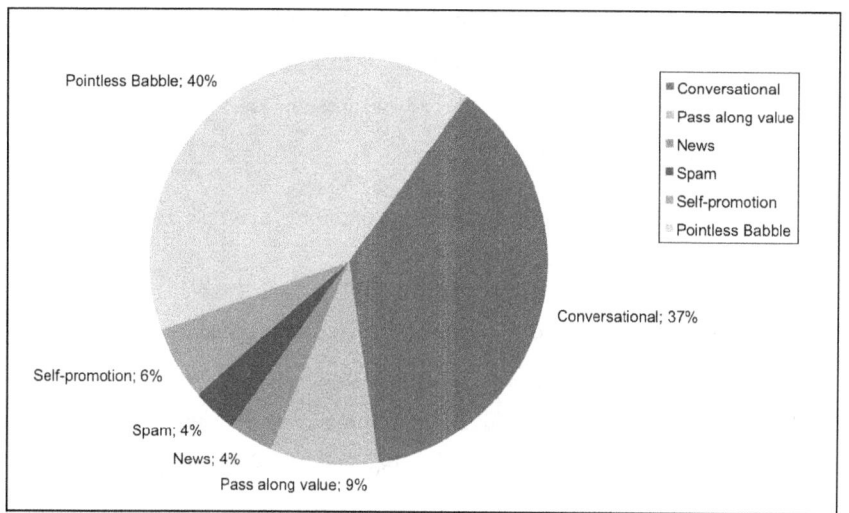

Source: Adapted from Ryan (2009)

Brick-and mortar companies as well as start-ups also use Twitter for marketing purposes. Several studies, among them the Twitter *Trendreport* by the communication specialist firm *Zucker Kommunikation* from 2009, conducted in 53 randomly chosen companies including almost 20 DAX or MDAX-traded companies, showed that more than 75% of all accounts have less than 629 following users. The follower average is at 661 with companies Twittering 13 times per week on average (Mai, 2009). Although this study is almost two years old and Twitter had just half the users at the time, it clearly proves that companies are "Twittering" as well.

Facebook

Facebook is a leading social networking site founded in 2004 by Mark Zuckerberg, currently employing almost 2,000 people (Facebook, 2011) and ranking as the second most visited website on the Web (Alexa, 2011). The service currently empowers more than 600 million active users to create personal profiles, add other users as friends and exchange messages (Carlson, 2011). According to *ComScore*, an analytics company, Facebook is the leading social networking site based on unique visitors, with over 130 million unique visitors in May 2010 (Prebluda, 2010).

Facebook offers further tools for steadily updating a user's entourage about news (updates) and locations.

The company also allows other companies to create profiles as a means of advertising and communication, and to update these profiles using its news feed application. Users can opt-in by liking these profiles and receive related updates in their personal profile news feed. For the scope of this study, several other functionalities offered to users are neglected in this description, as this paper's focus is on companies using Facebook, which do not use the mentioned functionalities. Numerous studies show the acceptance of Facebook among companies. A study, conducted by the University of Oldenburg together with the German agency *Constructiv,* shows that over 60% of all German brands are using Facebook as a communication channel (Horizont, 2009).

Weblogs

Weblogs, or short 'blogs', are a form of bidirectional communication on the Internet and proclaimed as one of the media of the future among the Internet avant-garde, bearing considerable risks but also opportunities for companies. To what extent Weblogs should be called a "secret media revolution" (Moeller, 2005) or whether blogs can be dubbed as "the new opinion-makers" (Zerfaß and Boelter, 2005) will not be discussed in this work. In their basic property, Weblogs are chronologically ordered, regular entries on a website, usually added by one single author and technically called posts (Ebner, 2005).

The high reach of Weblogs, as well as other social media tools, is produced by many links within and outside individual Weblogs and links of each website. The reader can be empowered through the opportunity to leave comments or references to the individual posts. The decentralized form of communication via Weblogs has an effect in two directions: first, it combines public and interpersonal communication, and second, it builds social networks. The exact number of Weblogs is difficult to identify. All sources refer to different measurement methods, relying on different demarcation and measurement problems.

Further, it is not clearly defined what characterizes a Weblog at all. Both in the activity levels, i.e. the frequency of use by the blogger, and in the variety of different types of Weblogs, these measurement problems occur (Schmidt, 2006).

In Germany, according to the *Allensbach computer and technology analysis (2010)*, approximately 8.4% of Internet users have their own Weblog. Worldwide (as of early 2010), there was a total of about 200 million blogs (Briegleb, 2010). The daily increment in usage does not allow accurate measurement.

2.3.2 Sample

The study focuses on German Internet and technology start-ups founded after 2004 and no later than 2009. The final sample of start-up companies participating in the survey consisted of 258 companies from the German technology landscape and is demographically diverse.

The author decided to research German Internet start-ups, as it was assumed that social media is a technology-driven innovation field and Internet and technology companies, due to their nature, are among the first to adapt those new media forms.

To explore the propositions in this study, the author selected all company start-ups that were founded after 2004 using public sources of information. He focused on start-ups being founded after 2004 because of data collection reasons and the fact that young companies' success is often not yet fully visible, and the right social media strategy might be one measurable success factor. A total of 928 start-ups were identified.

Those companies were gathered by using public databases available on German *entrepreneurs-focusing* websites such as www.deutsche-startups.de and www.gruenderszene.de, assuming that a start-up that was not mentioned there has not yet overcome the hurdle of raising general interest and lacks a clear visibility in the Internet scene in Germany. To validate that method, the author conducted in-depth manual research on diverse venture-capital data bases and venture capital web sites, analyzed their publicly deployed portfolio and cross-checked with the findings from this previous data gathering.

The author then deleted all start-ups from this sample database that were already trade-sold or listed on the stock exchange, or where founders had left the management, assuming that those companies are either not considered as start-ups anymore or that data collection would be biased. The sample decreased to a number of 775 start-up companies. In a last step, the author limited the size of the sample by randomly choosing one third of the start-up companies identified, equalling 258 start-ups that were invited to participate in the survey.

Regarding the chosen start-ups, founding management was selected as addressee. This was important to ensure that qualified answers were received with regard to certain financial questions in the survey.

The final sample consisted of 218 companies that matched the chosen eligibility criteria for this study and participated in the survey, which equals a response rate of 84.7%. The efficiency and cost side of social media further allows for gaining a market footprint without the investment of high amounts of money, and therefore ought to be very attractive in particular for start-ups whose financial resources are limited.

2.3.3 Procedure

Before the survey was released, a pre-test (n=20) was conducted to develop the questionnaire and refine the possible answer possibilities. The survey consisted of 7 questions with regard to social media, 5 questions with regard to the company and/or founding team, and two questions regarding the financial status of the start-ups. A company's financial situation was measured by pre-defined answer possibilities without allowing the respondent to comment on answers.

After the pre-test, another pre-test (n=5) was conducted to ensure respondents controllability of the online survey.

Online Survey

The study was conducted using a personalized web-based survey. The survey instrument included a five-point ordinal Likert-scale to capture data on the use of social media among start-ups. The survey was conducted from March 2010 to July 2010. A follow-up request was sent two weeks after the initial send-out. To ensure positive feedback, a temporary webpage explaining the survey was built and put online.

Crawled data component

As the researcher did not have access to data on the actual usage of social media through the questionnaire, he used – in addition to the survey component of this study – in-depth crawling and data mining techniques with self-developed algorithms to capture objective social media behaviour. The start-ups were not informed about the capture of their social media usage data to ensure a non-biased answering of the survey questions. The algorithm crawled, in particular, the start-ups' corporate social media profiles on Twitter and Facebook during a one-month period from July 2010 to August 2010. Additionally, through manual research on the companies' corporate websites and through Weblog search engines, the start-ups' Weblogs were identified and analyzed for blogging usage behaviour.

2.3.4 Measurement instruments

As this study is of an exploratory nature, the measurement items were mostly chosen for the first time in research.

To address the first question of general social media importance, the founders were asked to rank the importance of different social media platforms with regard to their business and marketing strategy. The author also evaluated the experience of social media per platform using several questions regarding general knowledge about these platforms. He was primarily interested in gathering a subjective self-assessment of start-ups using social media.

The second proposition was addressed through analysis of the real social media behaviour, using algorithms that capture the start-ups' usage patterns in social media. For the usage of Weblogs, the author was interested in the amount of Weblog postings. Twitter usage patterns were analyzed by counting the amount of followers gained as a result of usage or engagement. Facebook, due to its restrictiveness and data closeness, was just measured by counting the amount of fans gained, in absolute numbers. Twitter and Facebook were not measured directly by usage or activity (e.g. through messages posted), but rather by results. The author believes that usage patterns can nevertheless be directly correlated to the followers and fans gained.

To address the last question, the author developed a variable that measures start-ups' financial success. As non-listed companies tend to avoid publishing exact (financial) numbers, the author was unable to collect exact financial figures in the sample. To overcome this obstacle, the author asked start-ups to expose their financial structure and indicate their revenue life-cycle situation. The revenue dimension is – according to Murphy et al. (1996) – one of the most mentioned indicators of success. The degree of financing – according to Whippler (1998) – represents another very important input factor for a start-up's success, and was used accordingly as the second key success variable. Given the fact that 63.3% of the sampled start-up companies were not cash-flow positive, it can be assumed that external financing is crucial for survival. At this point, the author has ignored the date of founding because of the fact that all start-ups that were interviewed were founded within a very short period of time, between 2004 and 2009, and investment rounds within the Internet scene usually occur within six months of time, allowing each sampled start-up to receive a venture capital backing if needed.

The goal was not to show the different rounds received by start-ups, but to identify the degree of financing in form of total cash received, a measure that shows the start-ups' attractiveness and therefore the belief in its success. Based on the rating factor, a comparison to a company's financial stock value, the author developed a variable that reflects the capital infusion received by start-ups, the so-called financial value variable (FVV).

Figure 4: Derivation of the financial value variable (FVV)

Degree of financing	Financial value variable (FVV)
Start-ups that received at least family & friends investment or used own cash	1
Start-ups that received at least one business angel round	2
Start-ups that received one venture capital round	3
Start-ups that received a family & friends or business angel round and at least one venture capital round	4
Start-ups that received several venture capital rounds	5

2.4 Results

2.4.1 Descriptives

21.2% of the start-ups were founded between 2004 and 2006, 29.95% in 2007, and 28.11% in 2008, whereas 20.74% were founded in 2009. Most sampled start-ups (57.8%) were within the Internet business-to-consumer (B2C) sector, while 42.2% were business-to-business (B2B) oriented.

In geographic terms, most start-ups were founded in Berlin (30.4%), Munich (13.4%), Hamburg (11.1%), and Cologne (7%), with the others spread throughout Germany. Almost 68% of the respondents come from start-ups that were founded as teams.

The average size of a start-up was in the range of 6-20 employees. Nearly all of the start-ups were familiar with social media and used at least one social media platform.

2.4.2 The importance of social media platforms

86.7% of the surveyed start-ups value at least one social media platform as important, with only 47.9% saying it is very important. The majority of sampled start-ups (40.55%) rank social networks such as Facebook to be the most important, with Weblogs the second most important (16.13%). Just 4.6% of the start-ups completely ignore or rank the importance of social media platforms for the general business or marketing strategy as being not important.

Table 1: How important are social media platforms?

	No answer	\multicolumn{5}{c}{Importance level}
		not important				very important
		1	2	3	4	5
Weblog	0.92%	5.53%	17.97%	25.35%	34.10%	16.13%
Twitter	0.92%	9.68%	17.51%	27.19%	29.49%	15.21%
Facebook	0.46%	2.30%	5.99%	17.51%	33.18%	40.55%

A comprehensive importance of all social media platforms is rare, with just 40.09% of the start-ups naming all three platforms as at least important. This integrated social media importance is only seen in the group of "advertising" start-ups of the B2B sector. B2B start-ups generally anticipate social media to be less important, with 66.31% of B2B start-ups naming at least two social media platform social media as at least important, while 97.5% of B2C start-ups see at importance with at least two platforms. Geographically, and from the company's age perspective, no differences could be drawn.

Interestingly, there is a statistically significant relationship of social media importance and social media knowledge, as revealed by a Chi-Square statistical test ($p < .05$). 59.44% of the sample claimed to be at least knowledgeable about Twitter, 81.10% about Facebook, and 64.05% about Weblogs. This could indicate that a start-up is quite uncertain if it uses the right social media application strategy and therefore lacks an analysis of its return-on-investment, although knowing that – if applied in the right manner– it might be very important for its strategy.

In conclusion, 86.7% of all start-ups name at least one social media platform as an important tool for their business and marketing strategy, while 94.49% of all start-ups claim to have at least high knowledge of at least one platform. This result proves perceived importance of social media in general.

2.4.3 The usage of social media according to the perceived importance

While general importance of social media is widely very high, usage patterns are very different. On average, just 65.13% of the start-ups interviewed use a corporate Weblogs, 52.99% have a corporate Twitter account and only 41.93% a corporate Facebook fan page.

It can be assumed that several of the founders have private social media platform accounts that they also use for communicating about their start-ups out of personal technology relatedness. As those private accounts are not entirely dedicated to their start-ups, they were not analyzed in this research. This assumption aligns with the fact that 57.94% of the founders are responsible for their social media strategy themselves, and just 19.16% of them have contracted a dedicated outside expert in this field, or employ a dedicated social media marketing manager (5.61%). But due to the nature of a start-up, i.e. a lack of financial and time resources, it is obvious that even if they value social media as important, they lack a clear focus on it.

Regarding the average usage per platform, Weblogs are the least frequently used social media tool for updates. On average, a German social media start-up has published 21.57 postings over a period of 12 months. The median is at ten postings per year, indicating some start-ups proportionally using social media more extensively than others. Facebook corporate accounts tend to have 124% more fans than Twitter pages, with an average of 517 users following on Twitter and 1161.37 fans on Facebook.

Table 2: Usage patterns of social media among start-ups, based on founding dates

Start-up founding date	2004-6	2007	2008	2009
Avarage Weblog postings (last 12months)	25.5	19.2	23.9	26.84
Average followers (Twitter) gained	445	452	336	233
Average fans (Facebook) gained	2147	996	919	464

So far, the author has tried to evaluate the general usage of social media, e.g. postings on Weblogs, or its outcome, e.g. fans or followers gained, by analyzing profiles on Twitter, Facebook, and the operation of corporate Weblogs. Not surprising is the fact that start-ups engaging in Twitter and Facebook gain an audience over time.

The correlation of importance and the frequency of usage are of utmost interest. The author can display this correlation by drawing the following results on usage patterns in Table 3. The relationship between the importance and the frequency of usage is statistically significant when applying a Chi-Square statistical test ($p < .05$).

Table 3: Usage patterns of social media platforms by importance degree

		Importance degree to usage correlation (per platform)				
		not important				very important
		1	2	3	4	5
Weblog	Posts	6.00	2.78	17.13	27.66	35.00
Twitter	Followers	7.69	61.25	245.47	312.64	905.69
Facebook	Fans	36.80	144.23	64.86	235.54	846.08

The more important a social media platform becomes, the higher its usage. One could derive that the start-up implements the right social media strategy depending on its importance evaluation. This again proves that it is not important in which year the start-up was founded or which industry or part of its life cycle it is in. A significant correlation of importance degree and usage patterns shows that start-ups tend to focus on implementing the right strategies according to their subjective importance regarding social media.

A very similar situation can be observed while analyzing the relationship between knowledge and usage. This relationship is also statistically significant, as a Chi-Square statistical test reveals ($p < .05$).

Table 4: Usage patterns of social media platforms by knowledge degree

		Knowledge degree to usage correlation (per platform)				
		not important				very important
		1	2	3	4	5
Weblog	Posts	0.00	2.50	8.86	20.32	40.31
Twitter	Followers	3.33	40.74	122.92	225.35	809.44
Facebook	Fans	0.00	10.43	97.40	620.70	447.93

2.4.4 The usage of social media and financial success

First, it is worthwhile to take a deeper look at the financial demographics of the sampled portfolio. Therefore, the author analyzed the start-ups by evaluating their revenue situations. The following table shows their financial situation on average based on founding years and based on industries.

Table 5: Revenue situation as first success dimension

Revenue situation	Total sample	Year of founding				Industry-specific	
		2006	2007	2008	2009	B2B = 100%	B2C = 100%
No revenues yet	9.17%	2.75%	1.38%	1.83%	3.21%	8.51%	9.60%
First revenues	51.83%	8.26%	15.14%	16.97%	11.47%	52.12%	51.20%
Cash-flow break-even	17.43%	4.13%	5.50%	4.59%	3.21%	13.83%	20.00%
Ebit break-even	17.89%	4.13%	6.42%	5.05%	2.29%	22.34%	19.20%
No answer	3.67%	1.83%	1.38%	0.00%	0.46%	3.20%	0.00%

9.17% of the start-ups do not generate revenues at all, with 40.00% coming from the B2B industry and 60.00% focusing on end-customer businesses. The majority of start-ups, i.e. 51.83%, have already successfully launched their products and started to generate first revenue streams. Almost none of the start-up companies, i.e. just 17.43%, are cash-flow break-even, indicating that all of them demand new sources of external financing, although it is not clear if they lack capital due to the missing figures about their current liquidity reserves.

In a next step, the author was interested in the types of financing rounds received to measure attractiveness for investors, and by extension one dimension of start-up success (based on the ability to attract venture capital money).

Table 6: Rounds of financing received as second success dimension

Financing received	Total sample	Based on founding year				Industry-specific	
		2004-6	2007	2008	2009	B2B	B2C
Family & friends or own cash investment	64%	57%	68%	61%	69%	71%	58%
Business angel round	49%	59%	43%	50%	47%	51%	49%
Venture capital round	31%	30%	31%	35%	27%	31%	31%
Several venture capital rounds	20%	15%	18%	24%	20%	18%	21%

It becomes evident that almost half of the start-ups, i.e. 49%, have at least raised a "business angel" round, and therefore proved some degree of investor interests. There is basically no significant differentiation of investment interest by professional investments with regard to a start-up's industry spectrum, with 31% of all B2B and B2C companies receiving venture capital. Approximately one out of five companies receives multiple venture capital financing, with 31% undergoing one round of venture capital financing. That outcome shows that almost one third of the angel financed companies did not succeed in receiving further financing. Investigating the founding years, it can be observed that capital raising became more difficult by 2009, with 69% of all start-ups investing family and friends money and only 47% receiving business angel financing, compared to 59% in the period of 2004-2006. While 2008 and 2009 prove to be the years of more successful fundraising among venture capitals (24%) and start-ups raising multiple capital rounds of financing (20%), it can be seen as a signal that the start-ups of those years outperformed the ones of 2004–2006 and 2007, at least from the angle of attractiveness to investors.

As mentioned earlier, the author was not interested in the amount of capital received, but more in the identification of a start-up's success dimension in form of attractiveness for investors. The author therefore developed the financial value variable (FVV) based on the number of financing rounds received by start-ups, with FVV 1 being not very successful start-ups and FVV 5 being very successful start-ups.

Table 7: Derivation of financial success based on financial value, derivated from rounds of financing received

Financial value variable	Total sample	Based on founding year				Industry-specific	
		2004-6	2007	2008	2009	B2B	B2C
FVV 1 (not very successful)	29%	15%	25%	35%	27%	27%	31%
FVV 2	23%	11%	29%	27%	22%	22%	24%
FVV 3	5%	4%	2%	5%	9%	9%	2%
FVV 4	17%	22%	18%	16%	17%	17%	18%
FVV 5 (very successful)	20%	43%	20%	10%	9%	20%	19%

Table 7 shows the financial success of start-ups in raising capital. While more than half of the start-ups, i.e. 52%, were not very successful (FVV1-2), just 37% (FVV4-5) were successful in raising external capital. Again, an industry-specific view does not prove any significant differentiation with regard to the financial value, with start-ups being almost equally successful in the B2B and B2C fields of operation. An observation that can be drawn is that the amount of start-ups tends to have de-matured from 2007, with just 15% being unsuccessful in the period of time between 2004 and 2006, but increasing to 27% in 2009. Successful start-ups remain almost equally founded in the last years, with 17% on average being successful in terms of rounds of financing raised. From what was investigated, the author assumes that start-ups' financial value increases over time, as the percentage of start-ups being founded in 2004 to 2006 dropped from 43% to 9% in 2009. This could be aligned with the fact that start-ups need time to evolve and attract investors. Therefore, it is worthwhile focusing on correlating the financial value with the revenue situation of the start-ups.

Table 8: Financial value as success dimension based on revenue situation

	Financial value variable (success dimension)				
Revenue situation	*FVV 1*	*FVV 2*	*FVV 3*	*FVV 4*	*FVV 5*
No revenues yet	0.91%	2.29%	0.00%	2.29%	3.21%
First revenues	17.43%	10.55%	2.75%	9.63%	8.70%
Cash-flow break-even	5.50%	4.58%	0.46%	2.75%	2.29%
Ebit break-even	3.67%	4.58%	1.37%	2.75%	4.58%
No answer	1.37%	1.37%	0.00%	0.00%	0.91%

Another interesting fact to prove is that there is no statistically significant correlation between the revenue situation of start-ups and financial success based on the attractiveness to investors (see table 8; Chi-Square statistical test; $p > .05$). This fact demonstrates that the founding years, and therefore the start-ups' chances to be better positioned on their revenue situation, can be neglected. What is even more interesting is the tendency that the less revenues start-ups generate the more financially valuable they become in terms of attractiveness to investors. However, as the author has not investigated the accompanying company valuations, he cannot fully prove this relationship.

Initially, the author was interested in a comparison of success levels of start-ups using social media and start-ups not engaging in social media. He therefore correlated these two success dimensions, i.e. revenue situation and financial value, with the importance and usage level of social media.

Table 9: Importance degree and usage degree of social media based on revenue situation

Revenue situation	Importance degree			Usage degree		
	Blogs	Twitter	Facebook	Blogs (posts)	Twitter (followers)	Facebook (fans)
No revenues	3.15	3.65	4.25	14.89	868.05	360.00
First revenues	3.46	3.15	3.97	17.35	287.45	675.00
Cash-flow break-even	3.21	3.13	4.15	14.02	178.60	216.86
Ebit break-even	3.28	3.16	3.97	8.44	253.50	87.62

Table 9 uses the current financial situation, measured in the revenue life-cycle situation, and accordingly puts this variable into correlation with the perceived importance level of social media by start-ups' managements, as well as the actual and therefore objective usage patterns. The evaluation of usage importance of social media is almost equal no matter which revenue cycle a company is in. This proves that social media is being perceived as important by all start-ups the same way, and that start-up management does not assign social media importance any true revenue leverage. What is more important is the actual usage of social media depending on the start-up's current revenue situation. It can be observed that start-ups use social media less heavily (in terms of actual outcomes) when they hit the break-even compared to start-ups that do not generate revenues at all (analysis of variance, $p < .05$). In particular, Twitter is used more heavily (868.05 followers) by no-revenue start-ups than by start-ups that generate first revenues (287.45 followers). Facebook starts to become less important when start-ups become operatively cash-flow break-even. The same can be observed with blogs. All the data derived from the analysis statistically significantly proves that social media, no matter how important it might be, becomes less important or focused upon when start-ups gain profitability.

In a last step, perceived importance of social media and actual usage patterns with the attractiveness to investors were compared, assuming this dimension would best reflect a start-up's success dimension, as start-ups are not necessarily focusing on revenue streams within the first years of existence but rather on usage growth, i.e. user growth in social communities.

Table 10: Importance degree and usage degree of social media based on financial value as success dimension

	Importance degree			Usage degree		
Financial value variable (Success dimension)	Blogs	Twitter	Facebook	Blogs (posts)	Twitter (followers)	Facebook (fans)
FVV 1	3.54	3.32	3.90	18.18	303.53	378.54
FVV 2	3.32	3.12	4.06	7.80	244.83	754.55
FVV 3	2.50	2.10	3.50	4.40	50.6	158.75
FVV 4	3.34	3.43	4.10	11.00	714.01	662.07
FVV 5	3.65	3.12	4.17	25.00	183.03	133.91

The financial value variable can be interpreted as a success indicator rather than a success dimension. Again, no correlation can be found between the importance of social media and the start-ups' financial value, although Facebook and Weblogs tend to be slightly more important to start-ups that are financially more valued in terms of attractiveness to investors. Start-ups that are self-funded (FVV1) or business angel funded (FVV2) tend to engage in social media to a very high degree. This might be an indicator that start-ups hope to gain some publicity in reaching out to new investors and therefore value social media as an interesting platform. The further advanced a start-up is (FVV4-5), meaning the more venture capital money a start-up has already secured, the less social media is used. This finding might be interpreted to mean that young start-ups realize that social media attracts investors in very early stages, but its visibility becomes less important when the start-up matures. Both results are statistically significant applying an analysis of variance ($p < .05$).

2.5 Discussion

This study focused on start-ups from the technology sector, as social media itself can be defined as a new technology. Market adoption of new technologies is generally more widespread among visionary technology companies than among established brick-and-mortar companies.

Over the past few years, user-driven technologies, especially social media platforms, have gained substantial importance for business purposes. Collectively, these platforms have enabled companies to communicate with their stakeholders at very low technical, financial, and personal costs. The dominance of platforms such as Facebook and Twitter leads to the general perception of high importance. Sites not only incorporate means to connect with others and to publish content, but also redefine how communication is performed. Nevertheless, companies and research tend to overestimate the importance of social media when comparing actual usage patterns. This is basically due to the uncertainty and lack of measurement possibilities of the direct return-on-investment.

This study focused on the evaluation of social media usage of German Internet start-ups that were founded between 2004 and 2009. A total of 775 start-ups within the technology sector were identified, of which 258 were randomly chosen to participate in the study, with 218 actually responding to the survey.

There are five central findings of this study:

1. Social media is perceived to be generally important by more than 86.7% of all German Internet start-ups.

2. 78.84% of start-ups use social media platforms regularly, with Facebook and Twitter being the most important platforms.
3. There is a high synchronism between the perceived importance of social media and actual usage.
4. There seems to be evidence that start-ups that perceive social media to be important are at least as successful as start-ups that actually use social media intensively.
5. There is a tendency that start-ups decrease the use of social media with increasing financial stability.

In addition, this study shows that entrepreneurs are widely experienced in social media; almost nine out of ten entrepreneurs expressed either good or very good experience in at least one platform. The author further asked for the personal responsibility for social media usage, and found out that 94.39% did not have a dedicated person within the company following and implementing the right social media mix. This result is surprising in itself, taking the high importance of social media into account.

Even within the business-to-business sector, social media might be a worthwhile commitment. Technical issues and potential business partners tend to exchange ideas and recommendations among fellow industry thinkers in business networks and forums, allowing for an increasingly fast decision-making process (Gaffney and Ferrante, 2010). While most corporations have sufficient means to implement social media even without setting dedicated goals, start-ups – with their limited time and money resources – should evaluate strategies more analytically. A start-up should dedicate its attention to what provides the highest value. Another widely observed tendency is the trend factor of social media per se, and the fact that it seems to be basically free-of-charge. It can be implied that start-ups value this advantage and attach a paramount importance to social media.

Ultimately, research could embrace a more holistic view on return-of-success by using multi-dimensional success-metrics. Social media might have a longer-term perspective and therefore it could be interesting to analyze different key goal dimensions of its usage.

2.5.1 Limitations

There are certain limitations to this study, which need to be taken into account for future research. Obvious ones are the restrictions to just one geographical zone, one industry, and – even more problematic – one type of company, i.e. start-ups.

With regard to the importance of social media for marketing and business purposes, a clearer comparability of the sample would be eligible. The start-up sample was drawn from different intra-industry segments. They were also founded at different times, and most importantly had different goals at their lifetime-cycle position. Research might possibly solve this problem by focusing on a dedicated, self-expressed goal of social media. Start-ups might be asked whether the diffusion of information or consumption of information is preliminarily important.

One granularity may be the differentiation of audiences that are trying to be reached with social media, allowing for better comparisons of start-ups which are, for example, looking for new funding (VC-audience interesting), or start-ups already funded, looking for new suppliers or customers.

Furthermore, several widely accepted dimensions of social media measurement have been ignored. With regard to Weblogs, a differentiation of industries (B2B and B2C) would be as important as the measurement of the Weblog quality. Differentiators might include the goals of a Weblog (company-focused versus customer-focused), the amount of bloggers posting news, or simply its technical feature sets, such as mash-up integrations of Twitter or Facebook. Furthermore, the study completely ignored activity rates such as commenting or rating functionalities as a feedback channel. The major issue lies with the measurement of the audience. Readers or other web tracking analytics such as the *Alexa* rate, which indicates the potential reach of a website, hinders the author from monitoring how many actual stakeholders were engaged in this communication method. Trackbacks and other directly-to-Weblog software correlated functionalities might further help to measure viral spread of postings and would therefore be a good indicator of social media spread. Twitter also provides more measurement dimensions that were used in this study. As with Weblogs, the biggest problems arise from the missing measurement possibilities of visits or readers, especially as tweets can be re-tweeted by other users. The author completely ignored the company-driven proactive engagement in following other Twitter-users, known as following. As pure numbers do not indicate anything about the quality of the audience, it might be ignored in further research as well, but probably should be taken into account as a control variable. Activity rates such as the amount of tweets per week or response dimensions such as direct messages and re-tweets are of high importance to measure engagement levels. Viral aspects of social media, such as the spreading of tweets over multiple platforms, especially the ones directly connected to Twitter such as LinkedIn or Facebook, were completely ignored as well.

The author is also aware of the fact that measurement should focus on a larger time span, as 30 days might not be representative. As absolute numbers in followers were taken, the author tried to measure the attractiveness of a Twitter account as he assumes that a company that is successful in terms of social media attracts many users following its postings.

The author is aware of the fact that this exploratory study shows certain limitations; due to the nature of its focus, those limitations were deliberately chosen.

2.5.2 Future Research

Based on the findings of this study, additional research must be conducted to support the underlying results. In particular, the before-mentioned limitations on further success dimensions of measurement of social media should be taken into further analysis. Data used should be more dynamic and activity-centric, such as commenting and viral spread figures. In a further study, growth rates in numbers of fans and following Twitter users on both platforms could be correlated to either general platform growths or activity rates, messages posted or sent.

With respect to the first proposition of this paper, further research might also differentiate the levels of importance of social media with regard to the companies' strategic goals. The second proposition could be elaborated by measuring usage with regard to company perspectives such as goals of active information diffusion or more passive-orientated activities such as information monitoring.

Lastly, the author believes that there is also room for other success dimensions in this field. Success factors should be elaborated in more depth according to a company's perspectives set in a social media strategy. For instance, brand awareness or relative market share seem to be very interesting measurement dimensions.

Aside from the aforementioned criteria referring directly to the hypotheses, it can be assumed that further research should take a more micro-centric view by analyzing the social media responsible officer within a start-up. Research must consequently take into account the personal knowledge levels of the people or entities in charge of social media, including education and work experience as well as general company sizes.

Ultimately, a comparison among different industries and sectors is important to objectively represent social media as a success factor that is not limited to technology or media-orientated companies only.

Another interesting direction for further research might be the correlation to different corporate cultures and social media. As social media is inherited in the communication and marketing departments of companies, it would be interesting to observe how it fits different cultures.

Bibliography

Alexa Inc. (2010). Traffic details from Alexa, Retrieved on February 20, 2011, from http://www.alexa.com/siteinfo/twitter.com

Alexa Inc. (2011). Traffic details from Alexa, Retrieved on February 20, 2011, from http://www.alexa.com/siteinfo/facebook.com

Alston, D. (2009). Article on: Social Media ROI - What's the 'Return on Ignoring'? Marketing Profs. Retrieved December 12, 2010, from https://www.marketingprofs.com/

Blechner, N. (2011). ARD news article on social media: The New Regular's Table. Retrieved February 10, 2011, from http://boerse.ard.de/content.jsp?key=dokument_505616

Bolton Report (1971). Report of the Committee of Inquiry on Small Firms, chaired by J.E. Bolton, Cmnd. 4811, HMSO, London.

Briegleb, V. (2010). Article on: Medienexperte: Zeitungen werden verschwinden, Retrieved January 20, 2011, from http://www.heise.de/newsticker/meldung/Medienexperte-Zeitungen-werden-verschwinden-908468.html

Carlson, N. (2011). Article on: Facebook Has More Than 600 Million Users, Goldman Tells Clients, Retrieved on February 20, 2011, from http://www.businessinsider.com/facebook-has-more-than-600-million-users-goldman-tells-clients-2011-1

Cowling, D. (2010). Article on: Social Media Stats in Austrialia - Facebook Blogger, Myspace. Retrieved February 3, 2010, from http://www.socialmedianews.com.au/social-media-stats-in-australia-facebook-blogger-myspace/

Day, J. et al. (1998). Relationship Marketing: Its Key Role in Entrepreneurs' Long Range Planning, Vol. 31, No. 6, pp.828 - 837.

Debruyn, S. (2009). Article on: Measuring the Return-on-Investment of Social Media Campaigns. Retrieved February 25, 2011, from http://www.stephendebruyn.com/social-media/2009/12/28/measuring-the-roi-of-social-media-campaigns.html

Ebner, W. et al. (2005). Blogofy or Die, in: PR Magazin, Issue 2005, Nb. 12.

Eisenegger, M. (2005). Reputation in der Mediengesellschaft. Konstitution - Issues Monitoring - Issues Management, VS Verlag für Sozialwissenschaften, Wiesbaden.

Facebook Inc. (2011). Facebook Factsheets, Retrieved February 26, 2011, from http://www.facebook.com/press/info.php?factsheet

Fraser, K. (2008), Article on: The Evolving Nature Of Technology Adoption. Retrieved on March 10, 2011, from http://Weblog.getglue.com/?p=1090

Gaffney, A., Ferrante, A. (2010). A DemandGen Report, Whitepaper: Breaking out of the Funnel: A Look Inside the Mind of the New B2B Buyer.

Gruber, M. (2005). Marketingplanung von Unternehmensgründungen - Eine Theoretische und Empirische Analyse, Deutscher Universitaets Verlag, Wiesbaden.

Harris, A (2009). Article on: Contractors Market With Social Media. Air Conditioning, Heating & Refrigeration News from December 21, 2009. Retrieved February 25, 2011 from Research Library, ProQuest.

Hills, G. et al. (2010). History, Theory and Evidence of Entrepreneurial Marketing - An Overview, International Journal of Entrepreneurship and Innovation Management, Vol. 11, No. 1.

Hoffmann, D. (2010). Article on: Social Media Nutzerzahlen und Trends in Deutschland 1/2010. Retrieved February 10, 2011, from http://www.socialmedia-Weblog.de/2010/04/social-media-nutzerzahlen-und-trends-in-deutschland/

Hong, S., Yang, S.-U. (2009). Effects of Reputation, Relational Satisfaction, and Customer-Company Identification on Positive Word-of-Mouth Intensions, Journal of Public Relations Research, 21 (4). p.381-403.

Horizont Study (2009). 60 Prozent der deutschen Unternehmen nutzen Social Media. Retrieved December 15, 2009, from http://www.horizont.net/aktuell/digital/pages/protected/Studie-60-Prozent-der-deutschen-Unternehmen-nutzen-Social-Media_88992.html

Huesing, A.(2010). Article on: Facebook saugt die Konkurrenz auf - Stayfriends im freien Fall - Soziale Netzwerke im AGOF-Check. Retrieved February 15, 2010, from http://www.deutsche-startups.de/2010/12/16/facebook-saugt-die-konkurrenz-auf-stayfriends-im-freien-fall-soziale-netzwerke-im-agof-check/

IfD Allensbach (2010). Study retrieved February 10, 2011, from http://de.statista.com/statistik/diagramm/studie/22662/umfrage/betreiben-eines-eigenen-web-blogs-(online-tagebuch)

Kaplan, M., Haenlein, M. (2010). "Users of the World, Unite! The Challenges and Opportunities of Social Media". Business Horizons 53 (1): 59-68.

Keasey, K. and Watson, R. (1991). The State of the Art of Small Firm Failure Prediction: Achievements and Prognosis, International Small Business Journal, Vol. 9 No. 4, p11-28.

Kelly, N. (2010). Article on: 4 Ways to Measure Social Media and Its Impact on Your Brand. Retrieved January 2, 2011, from http://www.socialmediaexaminer.com/4-ways-measure-social-media-and-its-impact-on-your-brand

Kiellisch, T. (2009), Article on: Die wichtigsten Trends für 2010. Retrieved March 12, 2011, from: http://www.business-wissen.de/marketing/online-marketing-die-wichtigsten-trends-fuer-2010/

Mai, J. (2009). Article on: Corporate-Twitter-Studie - So twittern deutsche Unternehmen. Retrieved February 20, 2011, from http://karrierebibel.de/corporate-twitter-studie-so-twittern-deutsche-unternehmen

Mauro, C. (2009). Article on: What US Airways Flight 1549's Ditching in the Hudson River Teaches Companies About How to Create World-Class User Interface Design Solutions. Retrieved February 10, 2011, from http://www.mauronewmedia.com/Weblog/2009/04/what-us-airways-flight-1549s-ditching-in-the-hudson-river-teaches-companies-about-how-to-create-world-class-user-interface-design-solutions/

Möller, E. (2005). Die heimliche Medienrevolution. Wie Weblogs, Wikis und freie Software die Welt verändern, Heise, Hannover.

Murphy, G. (1996). Measuring Performance in Entrepreneurship Research, Journal of Business Research, Vol. 36, 1996, p15-23.

Neuberger, C. (2005). Weblogs verstehen. Über den Strukturwandel der Öffentlichkeit im Internet, in Picot, A., Fischer, T. (eds): Weblogs professionell. Grundlagen, Konzepte und Praxis im unternehmerischen Umfeld, Hannover, p113-129.

Nielson Report (2011). Article on: Social Networks/Blogs Now Account for One in Every Four and a Half Minutes Online. Retrieved January 9, 2011, from http://Weblog.nielsen.com/nielsenwire/global/social-media-accounts-for-22-percent-of-time-online/

Pfeiffer, T. (2010). Article on: Anzahl der Twitteraccounts in Deutschland, Österreich und der Schweiz (und Liechtenstein:-). Retrieved Frebruary 26, 2011, from http://webevangelisten.de/anzahl-twitteraccounts-deutschland-oesterreich-schweiz/

Prebluda, A. (2010). Article on: We're Number Two! Facebook Moves Up One Big Spot in the Charts. Retrieved December 15, 2010, from http://Weblog.compete.com/2010/02/17/we%E2%80%99re-number-two-facebook-moves-up-one-big-spot-in-the-charts/

Prescott, L. (2010). Article on: 54% of US Internet Users on Facebook, 27% on MySpace. Retrieved January 9, 2011, from http://digital.venturebeat.com/2010/02/10/54-of-us-internet-users-on-facebook-27-on-myspace/trackback/

Quantcast Audience Profile (2010). Twitter Growth. Retrieved on February 20, 2011, from http://www.quantcast.com/twitter.com

Rain, K. (2009). Twitter Study Reveals Interesting Results About Usage. San Antonio, Texas: Pear Analytics. Retrieved on December 15, 2010 from http://www.pearanalytics.com/Weblog/wp-content/uploads/2010/05/Twitter-Study-August-2009.pdf

Richards, R. (2006). Online Marketing Success Stories, Atlantic Publishing Group, Ocala, Florida.

Schmidt, J. (2006). Weblogs - eine kommunikationssoziologische Studie, UVK Verlagsgesellschaft, Konstanz.

Schulte, R. (2010). Entrepreneurial Marketing and the Role of Information - Evidence From Young Service Ventures, International Journal of Entrepreneurship and Innovation Management, Vol. 11, No. 1.

Smith, D. (2009). Financial Bootstrapping and Social Capital: How Technology-Based Start-Ups Fund Innovation, International Journal Entrepreneurship and Innovation Management, Vol. 10, No. 2, 2009.

Smith, T. (2009). The Social Media Revolution, International Journal of Market Research, Vol. 51, Issue 4.

Taxali G. (2009). Article on: Cashing on Tweets. Computerworld Magazine from September 21, 2008, p24.

Twitter Inc. (2009). Article on: There Is a List for That. Retrieved on January 15, 2011 from http://Weblog.twitter.com/2009/10/theres-list-for-that.html

Watson, K. et al. (1995). Small Business Start-Ups: Success Factors and Support Implications, International Journal of Entrepreneurial Behaviour & Research, Bradford & Leeds, UK.

Zerfaß, A., Boelter, D. (2005). Die neuen Meinungsmacher - Weblogs als Herausforderung für Kampagnen, Marketing, PR und Medien, Nausner & Nausner, Graz.

3 It is not only the investors' network, but the frequency of interaction between investors and founders that drives the performance of start-up companies

Authors: Matyka, D.; Jung, S.

Abstract

Past research found that syndication networks and the position an investor has within this network affects his fund performance. This is in line with general findings that network influences performance based on social network theory (e.g. information brokerage because of structural holes or reputation and trust issues). Beside this, the frequency of interactions between founders and investors influences the performance of start-up companies, as investors offer support and advice to their portfolio companies. Therefore, we argue that better network positioning of investors leads to better performance of their portfolio companies. This effect is moderated by the frequency of interactions between investors and founders, as the best network is of little help if no access to it is provided. Following these theoretical considerations, we conducted a social network analysis based on data from German commercial register as well as a subsequent survey of start-up founders. Our analysis support both proposed effects.

3.1 Introduction

The exploitation of innovative ideas and the creation of businesses lie at the heart of economic growth and technological advancement (Schumpeter, 1942). A better understanding of entrepreneurship and the factors influencing it are thus of vital importance. In today's economy, the role of new ideas, products, and services developed by founders of start-ups are seen as crucial for economic growth. In particular, high-technology start-ups, which constantly innovate, play an important role in the overall economy.

However, founders having bright ideas are only one factor. The other important factor that enables the ideas to be developed into real products and services is capital (Gompers and Lerner, 2001). For entrepreneurs, it is of the utmost importance to have access to sources of capital in order to exploit their ideas. In past decades, venture capitalists have developed as an important intermediary in financial markets (by providing capital to firms that might otherwise have difficulty attracting equity financing), and therefore play an essential role in the entrepreneurial process (Gompers et al., 2001). The importance of venture capital (VC) from an economic point of view is further underpinned by research that compares the success rate of venture capital backed companies with the success rate of new ventures generally and finds it to be significantly higher (Dorsey, 1979; Davis and Stetson, 1984).

In particular, the social network theory (e.g. Granovetter, 1973 and 1983; e.g. Burt 1992) has become one that is used prominently in entrepreneurship research. Starting with research done by Birley (1985) and Aldrich and Zimmer (1986), a long tradition of research analyzes the relationship between entrepreneurial networks and their effect on the success of start-up companies (Baum and Silverman, 2004; Hallen, 2008). The rationale behind this theory is that a network allows entrepreneurs 1) to obtain resources such as financial, production, or personal support at lower cost than on markets and 2) to secure resources that are not available on markets, such as reputation, information, or knowledge (Witt, 2004). Shane and Stuart (2002) found that the ability of entrepreneurs to establish direct or indirect ties with venture capitalists positively correlates with the ability to attract venture funding for the start-up company. More generally speaking, the social network ties represent the possibility to get access to important resources, as well as the potential to transfer these resources in order to create opportunities (Podolny and Page, 1998). Therefore, networks of entrepreneurs represent an important value for start-ups.

As venture capitalists help with operational planning and recruiting staff and offer strategic advice (Timmons and Bygrave, 1986), considerable emphasis has been put on understanding the nature and origin of networks venture capitalists form and make use of. Of particular research interest is the fact that venture capitalists are forming syndicates to invest or co-invest in firms. Hochberg, et al. (2007) analyzed investors' network positions and found that more central and thus more powerful actors in the network show higher success rates and higher survival probabilities of their investments. These findings assume that the pure existence of a superior network position of an investor is enough to result in higher success and survival rates of the respective portfolio companies. Nevertheless, as investors follow different investment strategies and therefore do not all allocate the same amount of time to each of their portfolio companies, these companies can only make use of their investors' networks according to the extent that they gain access to this network. This means that not only the syndication network position of investors, but also the willingness and possibility to offer access to this network to their portfolio companies influences the success rate of start-ups.

The aim of this study is therefore to shed more light on the role of these investors' networks in the performance of start-up companies. We focus on the networks' impact on start-ups, in particular by drawing attention to the possibility of start-ups gaining access to their investors' syndication network and not only to the shape and quality of the network itself. We propose that accessibility of the investors' network is as important as its quality. This is particularly important, as start-ups are advised to choose an investor and even pay a premium to investors that have high value networks (Hsu, 2004). The management implications of our analysis are twofold. First, we want to add to the choice set of start-up companies, focusing not only on the network of investors, but also on taking investment strategy into account when choosing the right investor, as the strategy corresponds with the time budget an investor allocates to each portfolio company, which has an impact on the venture performance. Second, venture capitalists who see their networks as an important market entry barrier (Hochberg et al., 2007) may look not only on the quality of their network, but also on the accessibility, as these two factors improve the performance of their portfolio companies and therefore also their own fund performance.

The paper is organized as follows: The next chapter gives a literature overview on syndication networks and their impact on start-ups, as well as the influence an investor has on his portfolio companies. Based on this overview, we develop our hypotheses within the next chapter. Hereafter, our research design and the results of our empirical study are presented. The paper closes with a discussion and conclusion.

3.2 Literature Review and Hypothesis

The quality of internal and external relations of a venture, i.e. the founder, management, and investors, is found to be central to a start-up's survival (Littunen,

2000) and has an impact on venture performance (e.g. Burt, 1992; Tsai and Ghoshal, 1998; Stuart, 1999). Firms that collaborate through partnerships, alliances, or investment connections benefit in three ways. First, they gain quicker access to information and thus save time. Second, they increase their own efficiency by better allocating their resources and therefore adapt faster to complex situations. Third, network organizations are particularly important in industries where knowledge is the main asset of competition and dispersal. Therefore, social network theory is of particular importance for start-up companies, which have to overcome liabilities of smallness and newness (e.g. Lua, and Beamishb, 2006) and therefore rely heavily on resources offered through their network (Witt, 2004). Two different schools of social network theory exist. On the one hand, the network closure is stressed (Coleman, 1988, 1990) by focusing on trust and norms that are built and could be sanctioned by networks (social control). On the other hand, the structural hole theory (Burt, 1992) sheds light on the information brokerage opportunity that arises from rather loose ties and the lack of network closeness.

The second theory is used to discuss networks venture capitalists regularly form and make use of – so-called syndication networks. They do so in order to share risk and obtain diverse information and knowledge (Bygrave, 1987; De Clercq and Dimov, 2004). According to Hopp and Rieder (2010), 75 out of 187 Internet start-ups are syndicated. Still, since about 1990 the on-going discussion on the reasons for venture capital syndication has not yet produced clear dependencies. For instance, Lockett and Wright (1999) contribute a study on the venture capital industry in the United Kingdom. Their results contradict previous empirical studies suggesting that the main motivation to syndicate is sharing and diversifying risks. In contrast, Bygrave (1987) argues that highly innovative and specialized firms motivate venture capital firms to form those syndicates and share knowledge and information to bridge the informational gap to the firm. Consequently, the investors can assess a firm's quality more effectively. As a result, investment decisions are based on the evaluation of different organizations. Studies conducted in Canada (Brander, Amit and Antweiler, 2002) and the USA (De Clercq and Dimov, 2004) support both arguments. Country specific differences provide a possible explanation. Europe's venture capital industry is characterized by smaller venture capital firms, having less than € 400 m capital under management (Hauswiesner, 2006). In order to overcome their liability of smallness, they are syndicating. Thus, they are motivated by the benefits of diversifying risks and having access to future deals. In North America, however, venture capital firms are larger (e.g. $ 2.5 bn. fund of New Enterprise Associates) and more aware of the importance of thorough selection and adding value to their investments (Manigart et al., 2006). Nevertheless, syndication plays a significant role in the U.S. Venture capital firms seem to prefer equally experienced investors as syndication partners in early stage investment. However, in later stages they are more eager to invite young venture capital firms into syndicates. This suggests that in early stage investments they rely more on access to other investors' resources, while they tend to share financial risks more at later stages (Lerner, 1994). Furthermore, syndication is more likely in earlier stages as outcomes are more uncertain (De Clercq and Dimov, 2010). To sum up, there are several different explanations why syndication exists and has become more important in recent years. 1) Syndication allows investors to diversify their portfolios on a larger number of deals (Manigart, 2006). 2) Syndication means information sharing between different investors and gaining knowledge from each other (Dimov and Milanov, 2010), and therefore reduces potential agency conflicts (Casamatta, 2007). 3) Syndication networks enhance an investor's deal flow, which enables him to fund more prospering companies within his portfolio (Hochberg et al., 2007). As a result of syndication, venture capitalists are interconnected by their shared investments.

VCs also take an active part in managing the company, as they often sit on the board and have certain control rights (Sahlman, 1990). In addition, venture capital investors supply their ventures with advice and information (Hellmann, 2002). Therefore, the network of an investor and especially the syndication network might thus have an impact on a venture's business activities, strategic decisions, and even performance. Or, as Lerner (1994) mentioned, by sharing their investments with other venture capitalists, risk sharing and mutual value-adding benefits can be generated. Venture capitalists collect information not only about but also for the start-up. This implies that they additionally intend to support their investments in terms of management advice and knowledge transfer. Firms that have received venture capital investment have been found to operate more professionally and practice market-oriented functions, such as marketing more intensively (Hellmann, 2002). Having access to the syndication network of the investor and particularly in the case of venture capital represents another advantage over other investors. According to theory and previous studies, relations are seen as vital instruments of information gathering and reassurance for entrepreneurs (Birley, 1985). Furthermore, since venture capital firms' performance derives mainly from their portfolio firms, they are inclined to pass on position benefits to their investments. Consequently, a powerful position of an investor within the syndication network is expected to relate to benefits for the start-up as well. To sum up, investors and their syndication networks influence a start-up's activities in diverse ways that lead to better performance: Firstly, the investor provides advice and key resources such as management expertise and skills. Secondly, the venture might have a better probability of securing an additional round of funding via the syndication network (Hochberg et al., 2010). Thirdly, an investor's status or reputation within the industry might strengthen the start-ups bargaining position. Fourthly, the knowledge and information investors collect are an important help and source of constant improvement to the start-up.

In line with the two main streams of social network theory ("structural holes" and "closure of networks") that are both said to support performance, we derive our hypotheses H1a and H1b, each focusing on one theory. Status, reputation, and a central position are factors that indicate an investor's relative power within a network measured by eigenvector centrality (Bonacich, 1972, 1987). Overall, the indications are that there is a relationship between a favorable venture capital network position and firm performance, which leads to the following two hypotheses in line with Hochberg et al. (2007):

H1a: The better the network position of an investor is with respect to its power, the better the performance of his portfolio companies.

While H1a focuses on the centrality and power an investor has within the syndication network, H1b sheds light on the extent to which an investor is bridging gaps between different investors (Burt, 1992) in order to function as an intermediary or broker by "bringing together VCs with complementary skills or investment opportunities" (Hochberg et al., 2007).

H1b: The better the network position of an investor is with respect to its ability to bridge structural wholes, the better the performance of his portfolio companies.

Research has been able to validate the value added to single portfolio companies by investors (e.g. Sapienza, 1992, 1996; Busenitz et al., 1997; Higashide, 2000). Nevertheless, there are also individual limitations of each investor regarding the possibility to add value. For example, the number of portfolio companies managed by a partner of a venture capitalist differs. Depending on the investment strategy of a venture capitalist, there is more or less time devoted to a single portfolio company. There exist several different investment strategies, which reach from "spray & pray" approaches to "company building" visions, from "active investment management" to "money is all I give" methods, that lead to enormous discrepancies in the allocation of time budgets to start-up companies. For example, a "spray & pray" approach tries to diversify investment risks by investing in many companies, which means the investment manager has only little support or time for the single start-up, while the "company building" strategy, where investors sometimes even start the companies by themselves, enables investors to give lots of support and advice to their portfolio companies, as they simply have a higher time budget for each investment. One of the most important findings of Sapienza (1992) was the positive effect of frequency of interaction between the investor and the founder of the start-up on the performance of the start-up, and we therefore propose:

H2: The higher the frequency of interaction between the investor and the founder of the start-up company, the better the performance of the start-up.

In addition to that, we suppose that the frequency of interaction also has a moderating effect on the main relationship of the network position of the lead investor and the performance of the portfolio company, which leads to the best result regarding venture performance. Our argumentation here follows a well-known theory on motivation (Martin, Seta, Crelia and Rick, 1990). The best results are achieved when ability comes together with willingness. As our first hypothesis reflects the level of ability of the investor to offer support through their network, and the second hypothesis stands for the level of willingness of the investor to offer support (Pullins et al. 1994), we propose that the combination of both leads to the best result. It is quite obvious that the highest quality network is of no or little value for the portfolio companies if the investor undertakes no or little effort to share the contacts with his portfolio companies. Therefore, we formulate our hypotheses:

H3a: The frequency of interaction between the investor and the founder positively moderates the effect derived from the better network position based on power.

H3b: The frequency of interaction between the investor and the founder positively moderates the effect derived from the better network position based on structural holes.

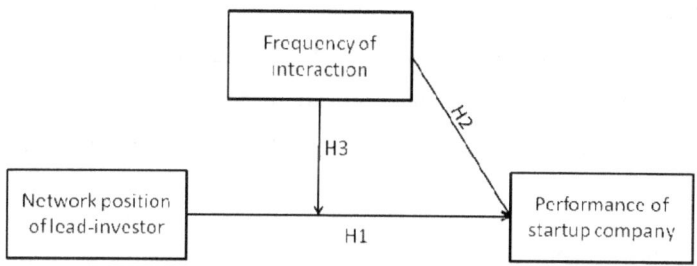

Graph 1: Research Framework

3.3 Research Methodology

Our research methodology is twofold. We first did a social network analysis of the German investors investing in Internet start-ups. We analyzed the syndication network of the investors at the end of 2009, based on all deals (active and exists) these investors closed since 2005. We also integrated the deals where investors already achieved an exit, as the connection to their syndication partners does not stop because of a successful exist (Sorenson and Stuart, 2008). Second, we conducted a survey study asking all founders of the collected investments about their relationship with their lead investors and some demographics on their start-up company in order to double-check our collected archival data.

3.3.1 Sample

As an empirical setting we choose the Internet industry in Germany, because it fulfills several important requirements for our analysis. With over 900 active investment deals (German commercial registry) from January 2005 until December 2009 executed by about 200 different investors, it is large and diverse enough to set up the syndication network of each investor. For our analysis, investors can be business angels, venture capital firms, or strategic investors (like media companies) who are part of the venture's entire network and are at least as important for start-ups as venture capital (Gompers 1995, p. 1488). Therefore, we summarize all kinds of financial resources for start-ups under the name venture capital.

Additionally, the whole Internet industry is rather new, with its second big wave after the burst of the Internet bubble in Germany starting 2004/2005 (O'Reilly, 2004), which means that all companies are of similar age compared to other industries and the deals are almost all seed or start-up investments. Furthermore, relationships between investors and entrepreneurs can be easily tracked from their very beginning until today.

As no databases comparable to US-based ventureOne (Reuters) or venture Source exist for the German market, we used the German Handelsregister (commercial register) to extract the syndication network of investors. The Handelsregister in Germany has to be informed by companies (especially limited partnerships) on any changes regarding the partnership structure. As almost all start-ups are founded as limited partnerships (95%), this register is an excellent source for all investment deals. Furthermore, we used public databases available such as www.deutsche-startups.de and www.gruenderszene.de, assuming that a start-up that was not mentioned here has not yet overcome the hurdle of raising general interest and lacks a clear visibility in the Internet scene in Germany. To validate that method, the author conducted in-depth manual research on diverse venture-capital databases and venture capital web sites, analyzed their publicly deployed portfolio and cross-checked with the findings from this previous data gathering. Additionally, we sent out a questionnaire to the founders of all 900 Internet start-ups. The survey was conducted from March 2010 to July 2010. Before the survey was released, a pre-test (n=20) was conducted to develop the questionnaire and refine the possible answer possibilities. After the pre-test, another pre-test (n=5) was conducted to ensure respondents' controllability of the online survey.

202 filled out the complete survey, which is a response rate of 22.4%. We compared this sample of 202 start-ups to the 900 start-ups in order to address the problems of biases that occur when dealing with survey-based research. Based on this analysis, we did not find any support for these biases (e.g. non-response bias or undercoverage bias) and therefore conclude that the sample can be treated as a random sample.

Year	Number of Startups	Branche									
		Sample									
		e-commerce	games	Music/Radio Video/TV	mobile	service software	social media	portal	search engine	marketplace	bankrupt
2005	11	1		0	0	0	5	1	2	1	1	0
2006	25	3		1	0	2	-	2	3	5	2	1
2007	64	5		1	2	3	17	13	13	3	-	2
2008	61	11		4	0	3	12	9	11	3	-	3
2009	45	8		1	1	1	12	3	13	3	2	0
SUM	206	28		7	3	9	53	28	42	15	19	6
Percentage		13.50%	3.40%	1.40%	4.37%	25.74%	13.50%	20.30%	7.28%	9.22%	2.01%
		Population									
2005	51	7		1	0	2	17	-	10	2	4	1
2006	115	14		3	2	5	17	17	19	11	-	4
2007	332	29		11	16	6	68	85	60	16	24	26
2008	258	44		10	5	10	42	47	65	13	19	15
2009	119	22		-	4	4	33	11	25	8	4	4
SUM	876	116		32	27	27	177	170	186	50	58	50
Percentage		13.23%	3.04%	3.05%	3.05%	20.16%	19.36%	21.18%	5.69%	6.61%	5.69%

Table 1: Sample and Population comparison

While the age of the population of the start-ups is 2.68 years, our sample of start-ups is slightly but not significant younger, with an average age of 2.49 years. The distribution between different sub-branches of Internet start-ups is also very similar, as Table 1 reports.

3.3.2 Operationalization

Syndication network

In this study, the social network analysis software UCInet is applied. It is considered to be a standard tool for social network analysis (Borgatti et al., 2002). Like Hochberg et al. (2007), we use the SNA measures "centrality" and "betweenness" as variables that show the quality of the syndication network a start-up company has access to. Wassermann and Faust (1994) and Borgatti, Everett, and Freeman (2002) describe the various network measures and provide explanations:

Centrality Eigenvector: Centrality in a network translates into access to exchange relations, bargaining power over other actors, and attention from other actors. Several measures exist that are considered to explain centrality in a network. It is a measure that calculates the network position of an actor in relation to other network actors and is based on the theoretical ownership of information. These measures have been used already in various studies concerning investor networks (e.g. Bygrave, 1998; Hochberg et al., 2007; Dimov, 2009). Besides including the geodesic distances of the actor to other actors, the eigenvector measurement puts more weight on a global sense of centrality within the network. It therefore reduces the impact of local environments and applies calculations that value the relative centrality to the overall centrality. This produces a more global view of an actor's network position (Borgatti et al., 2002) and also integrates the importance of actors an investor is tied to.

Betweenness: This measure is a proxy for the level of gatekeeping or information brokerage of an investor, as it measures the proportion of all paths linking actors that are connected through this particular investor.

For both *Syndication Network* variables we use the measurements of the respective lead-investor. If a start-up company has only one investor, than he is the lead-investor who is also in charge of the investment deal. If the deal is a syndicated investment consisting of two or more investors investing in one start-up company, there is always one lead-investor who originates and structures the investment deal. Because research found lead-investors to be the most active and important investors for the start-up companies that received a syndicated investment (e.g. Bygrave 1986; Birley, 1998; Gorman and Sahlman 1989), we took his network measures as the most relevant for this start-up.

Frequency of Interaction

In line with Sapienza (1992), this variable is measured by asking the founders of a start-up about the frequency of face-to-face communication and virtual communication via telephone or email with the lead-investor. We measured both interaction frequencies on a 5-point scale ranging from 1 time per year to 1 time per week and took the sum of both items as frequency of interaction. The mean of our data is 5.38, which means that the average frequency of interactions is about 1 time per month.

Performance

Since widely common financial performance factors such as sales, return-on-investment, and profits are not easily available from start-ups firms (Baumann et al. 2000), we decided to follow an alternative approach by using other variables that represent the performance of a start-up. These variables can be divided into two general groups, namely objective and subjective measurements (e.g. Mc Dougall et al., 1992; Chandler et al. 1993; Brush et al., 1992; Folta, Cooper and Baik, 2006). We used an objective measurement for our analysis and decided to double-check our results by also using a subjective measurement.

The growth of the organization is accepted as a valid objective measure of start-up performance. Furthermore, the growth of the number of employees represents an important aspect of organizational growth and is therefore seen as an appropriate alternative indicator for objective performance (Baumann et al., 2004). As our companies are rather young and cannot have grown large, the average number of employees is 2.3.

As subjective performance measure we asked the founders of each start-up to self-evaluate their performance in regard to internal development. To evaluate the internal performance the founders were asked to describe the status of their start-up, giving them 5 options: (1) We are pre-sales, (2) We have sales, (3) We are cash-flow break-even, (4) We are profitable, (5) We had an exist of our company (trade-sale, IPO…). Here, the average value of our sample is 2.51, which means that most companies are on their way to break-even.

Age start-up

We controlled for the age of the companies measured as time since founding, as a proxy for newness (average: 2.65 years). Age is also sometimes used as a survival indicator of young start-ups, which is also seen as a performance measurement. Within our analysis it clearly correlates with the number of employees a start-up engages ($r=.261$, $p<.01$).

Control variables related to the founder

As performance of start-up companies also relies heavily on the quality of the founder, we controlled for his education, age, and experience (e.g. Mc Dougall et al., 1992; Chandler et al. 1993; Brush et al., 1992; Folta, Cooper and Baik, 2006). We separated the experience variable into three different kinds of experience that are relevant fields for the development of a start-up company. We asked each founder how experienced in years he is within the branch of his start-up, his overall work experience, and his particular founding experience (novice or serial entrepreneur).

	Mean	S.D.	Min.	Max.	n
OBJECTIVE_PERFORMANC	2.30	1.237	1	6	201
SUBJECTIVE_PERFORMANC	2.51	.919	1	4	200
Eigenvector_LEAD	.054	.00	.00	.337	202
Betweenness_LEAD	1.58	2.63	.00	8.97	202
Frequency of interaction	5.38	2.38	.00	10.00	202
AGE_Start-up	2.65	1.297	.00	6	202
AGE_Founder	32.74	7.432	2	74	202
EXP_Founding	1.78	.795	1	3	202
EXP_Branch	2.60	.952	1	4	202
EDU_Founder	3.70	.881	1	5	202

Table 2: Descriptive Statistics

3.4 Results

Our findings are based on two different models we calculated. Models 1a and 2a represent the dependent variables that measure the objective performance of the start-ups, while Models 1b and 2b are based on the subjective dependent variable to proof the results of the main regression analysis. As the *subjective performance* variable is of nominal scale, we used a multinomial logit regression model (McFadden, 1982), while we used a linear regression analysis for the dependent variable *objective performance*. Models 1a and 1b are based on the independent variable Eigenvector_LEAD, while Models 2a and 2b are based on the independent variable betweenness_LEAD. We did this because social network measurement typically correlates very high, which leads to multicollinearity problems (r=.779, p<.001). Nevertheless, each of the network variables is interpreted in different ways, as they focus on different aspects and effects the particular network positions have (Wassermann and Faust, 1994). We first report our results based on the objective performance measurement and compare our findings afterwards with the results of the multinomial logit regression.

Throughout each model we found a significant positive effect of the network position of the investor on the performance of his portfolio companies. Therefore, we can confirm H1a and H1b. The better the network position of the lead-investor is within the syndication network, the better its performance. This holds true for better positions based on more influence and power within the network (*eigenvector*_LEAD) and for better positions because of a better information brokerage position (*betweenness*_LEAD). Also, our second hypothesis can be confirmed, as Models 1a and 2a show a significant positive effect of the frequency of interactions on the performance of the start-up companies (r=.129 (.133), p<0.5). This means, that even without taking the network position of the investor into account, a higher rate of communication between founders and their investors helps the start-up to avoid certain mistakes and perform better than start-ups with low communication rates. This positive effect becomes lower and is no longer significant as we analyze the mediator effect of the frequency of interaction on the correlation of network position and performance. This is in line with our proposed hypotheses H3a and H3b. The overall effect of the network position on the performance, including the moderating effect, rises from r=.303 to a combined r=.393 within Model 1a and from r=.241 to a combined r of .290 within Model 2a.

	Model 1b		Model 2b	
	Dependent Variable			
	OBJECTIVE_PERFORMANCE			
Independent Variables				
Eigenvector_LEAD	.303***	.170*	-	-
Betweenness_LEAD	-	-	.241***	.122`
Frequency of interaction	.129*	.076	.133*	.101
Control Variables				
AGE_Start-up	.199**	.188**	.156*	.187*
AGE_Founder	.056	.065	.048´	.057
EXP_Founding	.172**	.160**	.194**	.179**
EXP_Branch	.060	.076	.055	.054
EDU_Founder	.007	-.007	.031	.020
Interactions				
Eigenvector_LEAD x Frequency of interaction	-	.223**	-	-
Betweenness_LEAD x Frequency of interaction	-	-	-	.168*
adjusted R²	.223***	,244**	.188***	.195*
ΔR²	-	.021**	-	.007*

'p < .1 (one sided).
*p < .05 (one sided).
**p < .01 (one sided).
***p < .001 (one sided).
Note: Standardized coefficients are shown; n=202

Table 3: Results from the regression analysis based on objective measurements

Overall, our Model 1a (Model 2a) explains 22.3% (18.8%) of the variance, while the adjusted R² of the moderating Model variations is even 2.1% (0.7%) higher. Comparing the two dependent variables, *objective* and *subjective performance*, we find a significant (p<.01) positive correlation with r = .252.

	Model 1a		Model 2a	
	Dependent Variable			
	SUBJECTIVE_PERFORMANCE (Chi^2)			
Independent Variables				
Eigenvector_LEAD	7.295*	3.047	-	-
Betweenness_LEAD	-	-	6.033*	8.953*
Frequency of interaction	8.705*	7.697*	7.813*	7.658*
Control Variables				
AGE_Start-up	15.014**	14.288*	15.038**	19.673***
AGE_Founder	1.778	1.691	2.482	1.813
EXP_Founding	2.113	2.219	2.590	2.897
EXP_Branch	7.525*	7.616*	8.277*	8.442*
EDU_Founder	.956	.908	1.232	.849
Interactions				
Eigenvector_LEAD x Frequency of interaction	-	.388	-	-
Betweenness_LEAD x Frequency of interaction	-	-	-	10.371**
pseudo R^2 (McFadden)	.097***	.098*	.094**	.116***
ΔR^2	-	.001*	-	.020***

'p < .1 (one sided).
*p < .05 (one sided).
**p < .01 (one sided).
***p < .001 (one sided).
Note: Standardized coefficients are shown; n=195

Table 4: Results from the regression analysis based on subjective measurements (multinomial logit regression)

When looking at Models 1b and 2b, which are based on the subjective performance measurement, we find broad support for our results reported above. Apart from the moderating effect of the Model 1b, which does not exist according to this analysis, all other findings are affirmed. Table 4 describes the exact numbers and significance levels.

3.5 Discussion and Conclusion

In this paper we wanted to analyze the effects of the syndication network position of the lead-investor and his frequency of interaction with the founder on the performance of start-up companies. We found that both a better network position and a higher frequency of communication lead to better performance by the start-up company. Additionally, the frequency of interaction moderates the positive effect of the network position on the start-up performance. We therefore conclude that it is not only the quality of the investor's network a founder should look at when searching for funding, but also the investment strategy of the investor. If an investor follows the strategy of diversifying his investments as much as possible and invests in too many companies, he will have only limited time for his single investments. This leads to a worse performance of the start-up company compared to an investor who has enough time for each of his investments. Turning the story upside down leads to a piece of advice for venture capitalists and their investment strategies. It seems to be more valuable to follow investment strategies that allow the allocation of a certain amount of time to each portfolio company, as a better performance of the start-up should in the long run also lead also to better fund performance for the investor.

According to our results, it is also more important that the lead-investor has a strong network position than an information brokerage role. This means that for the performance of a start-up the knowledge an investor can provide because of his good information brokerage role is important, but even more important is the status and reputation an investor with a powerful network position can offer to the start-up company. This is in line with research on the price premium that start-ups are willing to pay for a highly reputable investor (Gorman and Sahlman 1998; Fried and Hisrich, 1995).

3.5.1 Limitations

Our research setting includes limitations we want to address here. First of all, the focus on Internet start-ups and a certain geographic region limits the generalizability of our results. Secondly, the performance measurement can only be a very rough proxy for the real financial performance of start-up companies. Earlier research legitimatizes the use of employer growth as a proxy, but real numbers on sales or cash-flow would be preferable. We tried to address this issue by also using subjective measurements to double-check our findings. That being said, we nevertheless think that our study is of particular value for the growing research community interested in the relationship between start-ups and their investors. Furthermore, we presented important practical implications for venture capital investors, as well as for founders of start-up companies.

3.5.2 Future Research

We suggest that future research follow two general questions. First, it is important to obtain a better understanding of which types of knowledge that investors share with their portfolio companies really drive the performance of start-ups. Is it a more general and process-orientated knowledge coming from heterogeneous investment portfolios, or is it the detailed and focused knowledge of one particular business model or branch an investor collects by having a homogeneous investment portfolio? Second, in line with our first suggestion, it would be interesting to study a phenomenon that we came across during our data collection process from German commercial register. It seems that a new type of investor evolves. These investors have recognized that their knowledge, experiences, and networks help them not only to support their investments and positively influence their performance, but also enable them to start their own companies. There exist a number of investors who seem to use their prior knowledge and experiences from many investments within one particular branch to take over the role of founders and start their own companies. Out of the 900 start-up companies we analyzed in order to build up the syndication network, about 15% of them were founded by investors.

Year	founded by investors	not founded by investors	number of startups	Percentage/Year
2005	11	40	51	5.81%
2006	23	72	118	13.44%
2007	74	258	332	37.81%
2008	46	212	258	29.38%
2009	32	87	119	13.55%
SUM	186	669	878	
Percentage	21.18%	76.20%		
2005	1	10	11	5.34%
2006	6	19	25	12.14%
2007	13	51	64	31.07%
2008	13	48	61	29.61%
2009	14	31	45	21.84%
SUM	47	159	206	
Percentage	22.82%	77.18%		

Table 5: Start-ups founded by investors

Vita Co-Author Stephan Jung

Dr. Stephan Jung works currently as investment professional at GCP gamma capital partners, a well-established and successful venture capital and mezzanine investor based in Vienna, Austria. Additionally, he supports startups and KMUs with his business modeling and innovation management expertise as an independent consultant. Prior to that he successfully co-founded a SaaS-Company in Germany, as Head of Marketing & Sales.

He worked at the Institute of Entrepreneurship & Innovation at WU Vienna as project manager of a European research network project (Marie Curie Program) and as Research and Teaching Assistant. The topic of his dissertation is: "From funding to founding - The changing role of investors". Stephan Jung is an active lecturer and coach at WU Vienna and TU Vienna. He studied at several universities including MIT Sloan School of Management, ETH Zurich and TU Munich.

Bibliography

Aldrich, H., Zimmer, C. (1986). Entrepreneurship Through social Networks. Ballinger Publishing Company, Cambridge, USA, 1986.

Almus, M., Nerlinger, E.A. (1999). Growth of New Technology-Based Firms: Which factors Matter? Small Business Economics, 13(2):141154, 1999.

Amit, R. et al. (1990). Entrepreneurial Ability, Venture Investments and Risk Sharing. Management Science, 36:12321245, 1990.

Amit, R. et al. (1998). Why Do Venture Capital Firms Exist? Theory and Canadian Evidence. Journal of Business Venturing, 13:441466, 1998.

Amit, R. et al. (2002). Journal of Economics & Management Strategy, 11(3):423452, 2002.

Jack, S.L. et al. (2005). The Role of Family Members in Entrepreneurial Networks: Beyond the Boundaries of the Family Rm. Family Business Review, 18(2):135154, 2005.

Baum, J.A.C. et al. (2000). Don't Do it Alone: Alliance Network Composition and Start-ups' Performance in Canadian Biotechnology. Strategic Management Journal, 21:267294, 2000.

Baum, J.A.C., Silverman, B.S. (2004). Picking Winners or Building Them? Alliance, Intellectual, and Human Capital As Selection Criteria in Venture Financing and Performance of Biotechnology Start-ups. Journal of Business Venturing, 19:411 436, 2004.

Bergemann, D., Heger, U. (1998). Venture Capital Financing, Moral Hazard, and Learning. Journal of Banking & Finance, 22:703735, 1998.

Birley, S. (1985). Role of Networks in the Entrepreneurial Process. Journal of Business Venturing, 1(1):107117, 1985.

Bonacich, P. (1972). Factoring and Weighting Approaches to Clique Identification. Journal of Mathematical Sociology, 2 (1972), 113-120.

Bonacich, P. (1987). Power and Centrality: A Family of Measures. American Journal of Sociology 92 (1987), 1170-1182.

Borgatti,S.P. et al. (2002). Ucinet for Windows: Software for Social Network Analysis. Harvard, USA, 2007.

Brush, C.G., Vanderwerf, P.A. (1993). A Comparison of Methods and Sources for Obtaining Estimates of New Venture Performance. Journal of Business Venturing, 7, 157-170.

Burt, R.S. (1992). Structural Holes. Harvard University Press, Cambridge, MA.

Bygrave, W.D. (1987). Syndicated Investments by Benture Capital Firms: A Networking Perspective. Journal of Business Venturing, 2:139154, 1987.

Bygrave, W.D. (1988). The Structure of the Investment Networks of Venture Capital Firms. Journal of Business Venturing, 3:137157, 1988.

Chandler, G.N., Hanks, S.H. (1993). Measuring the Performance of Emerging Businesses: A Validation Study. Journal of Business Venturing, 8, 391-408.

Coleman, J.S. (1990). Foundations of Social Theory. Harvard University Press, Cambridge, MA.

Coleman, J.S. (1988). Social Capital in the Creation of Human Capital. American Journal of Sociology, 94: 95-120.

DeClercq, D., Dimov, D. (2004). Explaining Venture Capital Firms' Syndication Behavior: A Longitudinal Study. Venture Capital: An International Journal of Entrepreneurial Finance, 6(4):243256, 2004.

DeClercq, D. et al. (2008). Firm and Group Influences on Venture Capital Firms' Involvement in New Ventures. Journal of Management Studies, 45(7):11691194, 2008.

DeCarolis, D. et al. (1999). Dynamic Capabilities and New Product Development in High Technology Ventures: An Empirical Analysis of New Biotechnology Firms. Journal of Business Venturing, 15:211229, 1999.

Dimov, D., Milanov, H. (2009). The Interplay of Need and Opportunity in Venture Capital Investment Syndication. Journal of Business Venturing, page forthcoming, 2009.

Davis, T.J., Stetson, C.P. (1984). Creating Successful Venture-Backed Companies. Journal of Business Strategy 5:45-58.

Dorsey, T. (1979). Operating Guidelines for Effective Venture Capital Funds Management. #3 in a Technical Series. Austin, TX: University of Texas.

Fried, V.H., Hisrich, R.D., (1995). The Venture Capitalist: A Relationship Investor. Calif. Management Review. 37 (2), 101-114.

Gompers, P.A. (1995). Optimal Investment, Monitoring, and the Staging of Venture Capital. The Journal of Finance, 50:14611489, 1995.

Gompers, P.A, Lerner, L. (2001). The Venture Capital Revolution. The Journal of Economic Perspectives, 15(2):145168, 2001.

Gorman, M., Sahlman, W.A., (1989). What Do Venture Capitalists Do? Journal of Business Venturing 4, 231-248.

Granovetter, M. (1973). The Strength of Weak Ties. The American Journal of Sociology, 1973.

Granovetter, M. (1983). The Strength of Weak Ties: A network Theory Revisited. Sociological Theory, 1983.

Granovetter, M. (1985). Economic Action and Social Structure: The Problem of Embeddedness. American Journal of Sociology, 91(3):481510, Nov. 1985.

Greve, A., Sala, J.W. (2003). Social Network and Entrepreneurship. Entrepreneurship, Theory & Practice, 28(1):122, 2003.

Hauswiesner, F. (2006). Venture Capital USA. Working paper.

Hansen, E.L. (1995). Entrepreneurial Networks and New Organization Growth. Entrepreneurship: Theory and Practice, 19·719, 1995

Hellmann, T. (1998). The Allocation of Control Rights in Venture Capital Contracts. The RAND Journal of Economics, 29(1):5776, 1998.

Hellmann, T., Puri, M. (2002). Venture Capital and the Professionalization of Start-Up Firms: Empirical Evidence. The Journal of Finance, 57(1):169198, 2002.

Hopp, C., Rieder, F. (2010). What Drives Venture Capital Syndication? Applied Economics. Forthcoming

Larson, A. (1991). Partner Networks: Leveraging External Ties to Improve Entrepreneurial Performance. Journal of Business Venturing, 6:173188, 1991.

Larson, A. (1992). Network Dyads in Entrepreneurial Settings: A Study of the Governance of Exchange Relationships. Administrative Science Quarterly, 37(1):76 104, 1992.

Lechner, C., Dowling, M. (2003). Firm Networks: External Relationships As Sources for the Growth and Competitiveness of Entrepreneurial Rms. Entrepreneurship & Regional Development, 15:126, 2003.

Lerner, J. (1994). The Syndication of Venture Capital Investments. Financial Management, 23:1627, 1994.

Littunen, H. (2000). Networks and Local Environmental Characteristics in the Survival of New Firms. Small Business Economics, 15(1):5971, 2000.

Ljungqvist, A. et al. (2007). Whom You Know Matters: Venture Capital Networks and Investment Performance. The Journal of Finance, 62(1):251302, 2007.

Ljungqvist, A. et al. (2010). Networking as a Barrier to Entry and the Competitive Supply of Venture Capital. The Journal of Finance, 65(3):829859, 2010.

Lockett, A., Wright, M. (1999). The Syndication of Venture Capital Investments. Omega, 29:175190, 1999.

Lua, J.W., Beamishb, P.W. (2006). Partnering Strategies and Performance of SMEs' International Joint Ventures. Journal of Business Venturing, Volume 21, Issue 4, July 2006, Pages 461-486.

Manigart, S. et al. (2006). Venture Capitalists' Decision to Syndicate. Entrepreneurship Theory & Practice, 30:131153, 2006.

Martin, L.L. et al. (1990). Assimilation and Contrast As a Function of People's Willingness and Ability to Expend Effort in Forming an Impression. Journal of Personality and Social Psychology, Vol 59(1), Jul 1990, 27-37

McDougall, P.P. et al. (1992). Modeling New Venture Performance: An Analysis of New Venture Strategy, Industry Structure and Venture Origin. Journal of Business Venturing, 7, 267-289.

McFadden, D. (1987). Regression-Based Specification Tests for the Multinomial Logit Model. Journal of Econometrics, 34 (1-2), 63-82.

Oreilly, T. (2004). What Is web 2.0? Conference Presentation.

Podolny, J.M., Page, K.L. (1998). Network Forms of Organization. Annual Review of Sociology, 24: 57-76.

Powell, W.W. (1990). Neither Market nor Hierarchy: Network Forms of Organization. Research in Organizational Behaviour, 12:295336, 1990.

Schumpeter, J. (1942). From Capitalism, Socialism and Democracy. Harper, New York, USA, 1942.

Shane, S., Cable, D. (2002). Network Ties, Reputation, and the Financing of New Ventures. Management Science, 48(3):364381, 2002.

Sorenson, O., Stuart, T.E. (2001). Syndicating Networks and the Spatial Distribution of Venture Capital Investments. American Journal of Sociology, 106(6):1546 1588, 2001.

Sorenson, O., Stuart, T.E. (2008). Bringing the Context Back In: Settings and the Search for Syndicate Partners in Venture Capital Investment Networks. Administrative Science Quarterly, 53 (2008): 266-294

Stuart, T.E. et al. (1999). Interorganizational Indorsement and the Performance of Entrepreneurial Ventures. Administrative Science Quarterly, 44: 315-349.

Tsai, W., Ghoshal, S., (1998). Social Capital and Value Creation: The Role of Intrafirm Networks. Academy of Management Journal, 41: 464-476.

Wassermann, S., Faust, K. (1994). Social Network Analysis: Methods and Applications. Cambridge University Press, Cambridge, UK, 1994.

Watson, J. (2007). Modeling the Relationship Between Networking and Firm Performance. Journal of Business Venturing, 22:852874, 2007.

Wright, M., Lockett, A. (2003). The Structure and Management of Alliances: Syndication in the Venture Capital Industry. Journal of Management Studies, 40(8):20732102, 2003.

Zucker, L. et al. (1996). Social Networks, Learning, and Flexibility: Sourcing Scientific Knowledge in New Biotechnology Firms. Organization Science, 7(4):428443, 1996.

4 Unsealing the relationship between entrepreneurs' success and their personality in the advent of web 2.0

Authors: Matyka, D.; Kratzer, J.

Abstract

The advent of Web 2.0 applications constitutes a new and potentially far more effective avenue for propelling new innovations and enterprises. Subsequently, interest in the relationship between personal traits and successful entrepreneurship has been researched in the last two decades. Our study bridges these two issues by investigating the relationship between personal traits of entrepreneurs and business success, the impact of utilizing web 2.0 technology on business performance, and finally the mediating and moderating role of personal traits on web 2.0 usage. A sample of 218 start-up companies from the German technology landscape serves as empirical base. Our results show that Extraversion and Emotional Stability have a direct and positive impact on business success. Likewise, the usage of the social media Twitter and Facebook increases business performance. And finally, Extraversion, Emotional Stability, and to some degree Agreeableness moderate the relationship between the usage of web 2.0 technology and business success.

4.1 Introduction

The interest in the link between personality and entrepreneurship has existed for some time. Research from the late 1980s could not demonstrate any consistent relationship between the variables mentioned (e.g., Brockhaus and Horwitz, 1986; Gartner, 1988). At the beginning of the 20th century, personality research has once again been included in business. Over time, there were several branches of research. Stewart and Roth (2001) studied entrepreneurs and managers with regard to their differences in risk propensity. This was followed by more general inquiry to identify global personality differences between those executives (e.g., Zhao and Seibert, 2006). Another line of research focused exclusively on the relationship between personality structure and the decision to become an entrepreneur (e.g., Brandstätter, 1997). The third major stream of research focuses on corporate success (e.g., Ciavarella et al., 2004). This line of research typically includes research on establishing one's own business because the first step to becoming a successful entrepreneur is to found your own firm. A meta-analysis of Zhao and colleagues (2010) summarizes several studies focused on the relationship between personality on the one hand and entrepreneurial performance on the other hand.

Our current study adds to this research stream by examining the relationship between the entrepreneur's personality and entrepreneurial performance. However, our approach is complemented by investigating mediating and moderating effects of the entrepreneur's personality on the usage of web 2.0 technology. Web 2.0 refers to the understanding of the Internet as a platform (Oreilly, 2007), which is reflected particularly in social platforms such as blogs, Twitter, or Facebook. The advent of Web 2.0 applications constitutes a new and potentially far more effective avenue for propelling new enterprises, and utilization of this technology might also be mediated and moderated by the entrepreneur's personality.

Our major question is whether entrepreneurs under the current state of personality do or do not have appropriate aptitudes for business success in the light of social media usage. To this end, we will attempt to challenge traditionally held assumptions about what our culture considers the ideal entrepreneurial candidate (insofar as their personality characteristics are concerned) and propose that new role models be considered based on their success and facility with social media. Since our study is one of the first addressing this issue, it is mainly exploratory in nature. Our examination contributes to the existing literature twofold. First, our investigation creates new insights on the mediating and moderating role of personal traits on the relationship between social media usage and entrepreneurial success. And second, the effect on different types of social media usage (blogs, Twitter, and Facebook) on firm performance is investigated. Subsequently, our study bridges the gap between research on entrepreneurial personality traits and research on media usage in the age of Web 2.0. The empirical sample of our study comprises German Internet and communication technology (ICT) start-ups founded after 2004 and no later than 2009. The final sample of start-up companies participating in the survey consisted of 218 companies from the German technology landscape and is demographically diverse.

4.2 Theoretical and operational framework

The Five Factor Model (FFM), a model of personality psychology, posits five basic dimensions of human personality. The origin of the Big Five began in the 1930s. Allport and Odbert (1936) found with a psycho-lexical approach the five stable, most culture-independent personality factors. Based on this model, the personality research developed further and today's internationally-used personality test NEO-PI-R was established in the 1990s by Costa and McCrae (1992). However, because it takes about 45 minutes to complete, the NEO-PI-R is too long for most research purposes and shorter instruments are needed. A number of shorter instruments have been developed to serve this demand. Among them, the well established, widely used instrument 10-item Personality Inventory

Measure (TIPI) has been created, which was applied in our study. To this point, dozens of studies have successfully applied this scale (e.g., Bear et al., 2008; Bias et al., 2010; Costello and Hodson, 2010; Ferris et al., 2010; Furnham et al., 2009; Geuens et al., 2009; Grant and Ashford, 2008; Hoyt et al., 2009; Ivcevic and Mayer, 2009; Li and Chignell, 2010; Mooradian et al., 2006; Motowidlo and Peterson, 2008; Poropat and Jones, 2009; Rentfrow et al., 2009; van de Garde-Perik et al., 2008; Xia et al., 2009). Because of the long history of development there is some disagreement about the Big Five's precise meaning (Barrick and Mount, 1991). In the present work, the following terms of expression are used: *Openness, Conscientiousness, Extraversion, Agreeableness,* and *Emotional Stability* (Gosling et al., 2003). Some scholars suggest that there should be another dimension called "risk propensity" to assess personality characteristics of entrepreneurs (e.g., Rauch and Frese, 2007). Due to the weak correlation between firm performance and risk propensity in the meta-analysis of Zhao and colleagues (2010), however, we did not include risk propensity in our study. We assume that risk propensity is reflected in the specific combination of the present personality characteristics (Nicholson et al., 2005).

Social media represents a rather new trend. In 2008, 75% of all Internet users used social media as a sharing platform. There are various approaches for defining social media that are mostly identical in content. We refer to the definition of Kaplan and Haenlein (2010), "Social media is a group of Internet-based applications that build on the ideological and technological foundations of Web 2.0 and that allow the creation and exchange of User Generated Content." User Generated Content describes forms of media content created by end-users that are publicly available (Kaplan and Haenlein, 2010). Probably the best-known examples are Facebook and Twitter. For all intents and purposes, the platforms dealt with in our study are blogs, mircoblogs (Twitter), and social networking sites (Facebook). The research in social media has evolved tremendously in recent years. Facebook as a social network has more than 500 million active users (Facebook, 2011), and companies worldwide quickly recognized the advertising potential of this platform. Particularly in marketing, interest in social media is large and the research does not end by any means in this regard (e.g., Rossmann, 2010; Mangold and Faulds 2009).

A company's success can be tied to different parameters. Current indicators are firm survival (e.g., Ciaverella et al., 2004), growth (e.g., Lee and Tsang, 2001) or economic indicators such as profitability (Zhao et al., 2010). The following study exclusively investigates growth characteristics (e.g., number customers) and the magnitude of venture capital that has been received as criteria for performance. In the latter case, venture capital is a legitimate indicator of performance because if financiers are willing to invest in a company, than it stands to reason that the respective company already performs well.

Figure 1 illustrates our conceptual model. First, we propose a direct relationship between certain personality traits and entrepreneurial success. Second, we assume that there is a direct relationship between social media usage and the performance of the new ventures. Third, we propose a mediating effect between certain personality traits and entrepreneurial performance. In other words, we assume that certain effects between social media usage and entrepreneurial performance are weakened, strengthened, appearing or disappearing when considering personal traits in the same model. And finally, fourth, we expect moderating effects between social media usage, personality traits, and entrepreneurial success. In other words, we expect that the mutual effect of certain personality traits and social media usage is stronger, weaker, or inverse than the sum of the single effects.

Figure 1: Conceptual Design

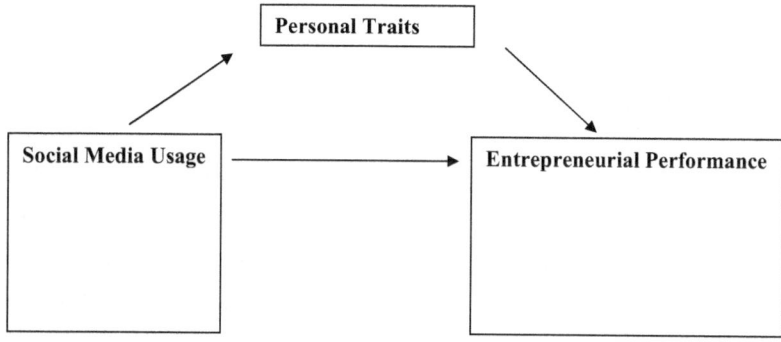

4.3 Hypotheses

Openness is a personality trait that describes someone who is attentive to inner feelings, intellectually curious, and tends to seek new experiences with preference for variety (Costa and McCrae, 1992). Openness is positively correlated with intelligence, particularly intelligence related to creativity, as measured by tests of divergent thinking (McCrae, 1987).

Joseph Schumpeter (1939) coined the term innovation in his analysis of the capitalist process. Short-term monopoly profits are the driving forces behind an innovative entrepreneur. The creation of something novel requires a high degree of creativity, especially in the initial phase of entrepreneurship. It is essential for success to be open for new ideas (Morrison, 1997). Moreover, Openness is related to performance in learning situations (Barrick and Mount, 1991). The leadership of a successful company requires constant adaptation to its dynamic environment. This adaptation is only possible if right decisions are executed and the consequences of those decisions are predicted. Making the right decisions is quite hard to learn, as you do not have experience to rely upon. Only when one has experiences to learn from can one handle new challenges more efficiently when one is confronted with them. So having a business requires a continuous learning process, and entrepreneurs who learn better will be more successful. For these two reasons, we expect a positive link between openness and entrepreneurial performance.

Hypothesis 1: Openness is positively related to entrepreneurial performance

Conscientiousness indicates an individual's degree of organization and need for achievement. It includes elements such as self-discipline and carefulness, and is an indicator of an ability to work hard (Barrick and Mount, 1991). Many scholars regard Conscientiousness as the most important personality trait for good job performance, and as the primary work motivation variable (e.g., Barrick and Mount, 1991; Gellatly, 1996). In short, this trait is described as necessary for entrepreneurs to ensure a successful result.

Hypothesis 2: Conscientiousness is positively related to entrepreneurial performance

Extraversion describes activity and interpersonal behavior. People with high extraversion values are sociable, talkative, person-oriented, warm, optimistic, and enthusiastic. They are also receptive to ideas and emotions (Costa and McCrae, 1992). Markman and Baron (2003) mentioned the importance of building networks with suppliers and customers in an industry. There will be a positive effect of extraversion for implementing required social interaction. A meta-analytic study of Judge et al (2002) shows Extraversion to be the strongest personality predictor of leadership. Because of these findings, we expect a positive effect on firm performance (Zhao et al., 2010).

Hypothesis 3: Extraversion is positively related to entrepreneurial performance

Agreeableness is also a dimension which describes interpersonal behavior, and more specifically refers to a tendency to be pleasant in social situations. A key feature is the expression of altruism. Individuals high on Agreeableness are characterized as helpful, empathetic, considerate, and friendly (Graziano and Eisenberg, 1997). Some studies have pointed out that agreeableness is particularly suitable for the attraction of venture capital (e.g., Cable and Shane, 1997), and therefore a critical element of entrepreneurial success. Nevertheless, a certain degree of selfishness and skepticism seems to be an important attribute if one is to be competitive. In accordance with Zhao and Seibert (2006), a negative relationship can be anticipated.

Hypothesis 4: Agreeableness is negatively related to entrepreneurial performance

Emotional Stability refers to an individual trait that enables one to have appropriate feelings about common experiences and to act in a rational manner. Emotional stability can help to increase self-esteem and self-image. Individuals who are less emotionally stable are more reactive to stress and less stress enduring. Meta-analytical findings show that there is a positive relationship between emotional stability and leadership effectiveness (Judge et al., 2002). Moreover, emotional stability is positively related to job performance (Barrick et al., 2001), and for this reason we expect emotional stability to also be a strong indicator of success for the average entrepreneur.

Hypothesis 5: Emotional Stability is positively related to entrepreneurial performance

Social Media empowers companies not only to communicate with their stakeholders, but also to excel in marketing, recruiting employers, and including customers in development. In conclusion, there are a wide range of new opportunities that are essential for being competitive in a global market. Thus, it can be expected that utilizing the possibilities of social media is a pre-condition for being successful as an entrepreneur in today's market.

Hypothesis 6: Social media usage has a positive influence on entrepreneurial performance

Due to the novelty of social media, it should be assumed that, in particular, those people who are open to experience use it more frequently. Finally, a study found that those who were more regular users of social media were also more open to experience (Ross et al., 2009). The question of whether a person's conscientiousness relates to the use of social media is complicated. We assume that a high level of conscientiousness results in more efficient use of social media. In other words, this means that the company will not use social media at the expense of other important business activities. Early studies showed that there were more introverted people using social media. It was thought that the anonymity of the Internet in particular drew the attention of these people (Amichai-Hamburger et al., 2002). More recent studies show different relationships, particularly in social networks. This may be due to the fact that many social media, though not all, in fact lend themselves to more public forms of social interaction (Correa et al., 2010). Landers and Lounsbury (2006) describe individuals with a low score on agreeableness as socially incompetent. For this reason, they have difficulty in forming friendships and try to compensate by using social networks. The use of social media enables communication on an entirely new level. This communication does not require face-to-face contact and therefore is interesting for shy people. In general, persons that are low in emotional stability demonstrate strong interest in using social media (Ross et al., 2009).

These findings demonstrate that the usage of social media may be personality dependent. Certain individual traits may stimulate efficient social media usage others do not. Thus, the relationship between social media usage and entrepreneurial success may be mediated by the personality of the entrepreneurs. It is reasonable to assume that, for example, the positive effect of social media usage on entrepreneurial success is reduced or disappears alongside trait openness. Due to the inherent and rapid availability of new and various information and experiences that can be easily consumed, the individual trait openness may be less deciding. Another example may be agreeableness. Web 2.0 technologies multiply opportunities for communication and in turn multiply the tendency to be pleasant in social situations.

Hypothesis 7: The relationship between personality traits and entrepreneurial performance is mediated by social media usage

The direct effects of personality traits and social media usage on entrepreneurial success are hypothesized above. However, it may be that the product of two single effects may be larger or direction-changing than two single effects. Social media diffuse personality traits very rapidly, so it may be, for example, that openness only positively affects the entrepreneur's firm performance alongside the usage of social media, or that the individual tendency to be pleasant in social situations may be disastrous for entrepreneurs when diffusing through the social web. In fact, it may be that only the combination of this personal trait and intensive social media usage elicit effects on entrepreneurial performance that cannot be found when looking at the single variables.

Hypothesis 8: The relationship between personality traits and entrepreneurial performance is moderated by social media usage

4.4 Method

4.4.1 Sample

The study focuses on German Internet and technology start-ups founded after 2004 and no later than 2009. Before the survey was released, a pre-test (n=20) was conducted to develop the questionnaire and refine the measurements. After the pre-test, another pre-test (n=5) was conducted to ensure respondents' controllability of the online survey. The study was conducted using a personalized web-based survey. The survey was conducted from March 2010 to July 2010. A follow-up request was sent two weeks after the initial send-out. To ensure positive feedback, a temporary webpage explaining the survey was built and put online. The final sample of start-up companies participating in the survey consisted of 258 companies from the German technology landscape and was demographically diverse. To explore and test the hypotheses in this study, we selected all company start-ups that were founded after 2004 using public sources of information such as www.deutsche-start-ups.de, www.gruenderszene.de. This was done assuming that a start-up that was not mentioned there has not yet overcome the hurdle of raising general interest and therefore lacks a clear visibility in the Internet scene in Germany. The study focused on start-ups being founded after 2004 because of the fact that young companies' success is yet not fully visible and the right social media strategy might be one measurable success factor. A total of 928 start-ups were identified. To validate that method, we conducted in-depth manual research on diverse venture capital databases and venture capital web sites, analyzed their publicly deployed portfolios, and cross-checked with the findings from this previous data gathering.

After identification we deleted all start-ups from this sample database that were already trade-sold or listed on the stock exchange, or where founders had left the management, assuming that those companies are either not considered to be start-ups anymore or that data collection would be biased. The sample decreased to a number of 775 start-up companies. In a last step, we limited the size of addressable start-ups by randomly choosing one third of the start-up companies identified, equalling 258 start-ups that were invited to participate in the survey.

Regarding the chosen start-ups, founding management was selected as addressee. This was important to ensure that we received qualified answers.

The final sample consisted of 218 companies that matched the chosen eligibility criteria for this study and participated in the survey, which equals a response rate of 84.7%. The efficiency and cost side of social media further allows for gaining a market footprint without the investment of high amounts of money, and therefore ought to be very attractive in particular for start-ups whose financial resources are limited.

4.4.2 Measuring Personal Traits

In this study we apply the Big Five framework that enjoys increasing support and has become the most widely used and extensively researched model of personality (for reviews; John and Srivastava, 1999; McCrae and Costa, 1999, Gosling et al., 2003). The Big Five framework is a hierarchical model of personality traits that measures personality at the broadest level of abstraction. Each bipolar factor (e.g. Extraversion vs. Introversion) summarizes several more specific sub-factors (e.g. sociability), which in turn subsume a large number of even more specific traits (e.g. outgoing). The Big Five framework proposes that most individual differences in human personality can be classified into five broad, empirically derived domains (Gosling et al., 2003). In our study we apply the Ten Item Personality Inventory Measure (TIPI). As Gosling et al. (2003) show, this 10-item scale reaches adequate levels in terms of (a) convergence with widely used Big Five measures in self, observer, and peer reports, (b) test-retest reliability, (c) patterns of predicted external correlates, and (d) convergence between self and observer ratings. All participants were asked to indicate the extent to which they agree or disagree with the following statements along the scale 1 = Disagree strongly; 2 = Disagree moderately; 3 = Disagree a little; 4 = Neither agree nor disagree; 5 = Agree a little; 6 = Agree moderately; 7 = Agree strongly.

I see myself as:

1. _____ Extraverted, enthusiastic.

2. _____ Critical, quarrelsome.

3. _____ Dependable, self-disciplined.

4. _____ Anxious, easily upset.

5. _____ Open to new experiences, complex.

6. _____ Reserved, quiet.

7. _____ Sympathetic, warm.

8. _____ Disorganized, careless.

9. _____ Calm, emotionally stable.

10. _____ Conventional, uncreative.

The TIPI scale scoring can be derived for the five personality traits by in the following way: *Extraversion*: 1, 6R; *Agreeableness*: 2R, 7; *Conscientiousness*; 3, 8R; *Emotional Stability*: 4R, 9; *Openness to Experiences*: 5, 10R ("R" denotes reverse-scored items).

4.4.3 Social Media Usage

Recent years have witnessed the rise of both Twitter as a social communication platform and Facebook as a social networking platform. Alongside corporate blogs, this new media currently belongs to the most popular new media tools. All of the three media can be seen as communication platforms allowing for user communication in a reciprocal way, acting as content creators and content consumers.

As we did not have access to data on the actual usage of social media through the questionnaire, we used – in addition to the survey component of this study – in-depth crawling and data mining techniques with self-developed algorithms to capture objective social media behaviour. The start-ups were not informed about the capture of their social media usage data to ensure a non-biased answering of the survey questions. The algorithm crawled, in particular, the start-ups' corporate social media profiles on Twitter and Facebook during a one-month period from July 2010 to August 2010. Additionally, through manual research on the companies' corporate websites and through Weblog search engines, the start-ups' Weblogs were identified and analyzed for blogging usage behaviour. For the usage of Weblogs, there we were interested in the amount of Weblog postings. Twitter usage patterns were analyzed by counting the amount of followers gained as a result of usage or engagement. Facebook, due to its restrictiveness and data closeness, was simply measured by counting the amount of fans gained, in absolute numbers. Twitter and Facebook were not measured directly by their usage or activity (e.g. through messages posted), but rather by their results. However, we believe that usage patterns can be directly correlated to the followers and fans gained.

4.4.4 Entrepreneurial Performance

In order to measure the entrepreneurial performance, two indications were combined: the financial success and the number of customers. As non-listed companies tend to avoid publishing exact (financial) numbers it is very difficult to reveal this information. To overcome this obstacle we asked start-ups to expose their financial structure and indicate their revenue life-cycle situation. The revenue dimension is – according to Murphy et al. (1996) – one of the most mentioned indicators of success. The degree of financing – according to Whippler (1998) – represents another very important input factor for a start-up's success and was used accordingly as the second key success variable. The goal was to identify the degree of financing in form of total cash received, a measure that shows the start-ups' attractiveness and therefore the belief in its success. Based on the rating factor, a comparison to a company's financial stock value, we developed a variable that reflects the capital infusion received by start-ups, the so-called financial value variable (FVV).

Figure 2: Derivation of the financial value variable (FVV)

Degree of financing	Financial value variable (FVV)
Start-ups that received at least family & friends investment or used own cash	1
Start-ups that received at least one business angel round	2
Start-ups that received one venture capital round	3
Start-ups that received a family & friends or business angel round and at least one venture capital round	4
Start-ups that received several venture capital rounds	5

The number of customers was measured along the 5-point scales from 1 – relatively little – to 5 relatively many – based on the question: How many customers does your enterprise have (a) in relation to the largest German competitor and (b) in relation to the largest international competitor? These scales were finally integrated into one scale and combined with the financial value variable into one scale of entrepreneurial performance.

Self-reported measures are often criticized in literature on adults, mainly with the argument that some people are unable to report their performance accurately due to poor introspection (Locke, Latham, and Erez 1988). However, there are also many studies that use self-reported measures and achieve high levels of accuracy (Cooper 1981). Moreover, there is evidence that self-ratings correlate highly with more "objective" measures in cases where anonymity is assured. In particular, Heneman (1974) found that self-reported measures were less restricted in range and leniency than the purportedly more objective ratings. Accordingly, we also promised anonymity in our study. In addition, Corey (1971) and Tittle and Hill (1967) argue that the error arising from self-reporting techniques is minor.

4.4.5 Analytical Techniques

In order to test the hypothesis we applied latent class regression analyses. We used latent class analysis because it offers fundamental advantages over traditional types of regression analysis (Vermunt and Magidson, 2002; Vermunt, 2003; Bouwmeester et al., 2004). Latent class regressions relax the assumption that the same model holds for all cases – in other words, the population does not need to be homogeneous as a precondition for traditional methods. A second advantage is that latent class regressions accommodate dependent and independent variables that are continuous, categorical (binary, polytomous nominal or ordinal), binomial counts, or poisson counts. As model fit we used the 2-log Likelihood, the Bayesian Information Criterion (BIC), and the overall R^2 as proxy for the explained variance. We tested mediation and moderation hypotheses with latent class regression analysis following Baron and Kenny (1986). A variable is considered as mediator when four conditions are met: (1) the independent variable should have a significant relation to the outcome, (2) the independent variable should have a significant relationship to the mediator, (3) the mediator should have a significant relationship to the outcome, and (4) when the mediator is specified in the full model, the relationship of the independent variable to the outcome should become non-significant. Before conducting regression analysis we examined residual plots and collinearity diagnostics. In the first step we included the variables on personality traits and contrasted them with the no-predictor model. In the second step we included the variables on social media usage. In the next steps we include the variables on social media usage together with the variables on personality traits in order to examine mediating effects. And finally, we molded interaction terms of social media usage and personality traits to test for moderating effect. Table 1 illustrates the descriptive statistics of the variables.

Table 1: Descriptive Statistics

	Mean	SD	2	3	4	5	6	7	8	9
1. Extraversion	5.33	1.12	.03	.06	.15**	-.62**	.14*	.11*	.13*	.08
2. Agreeableness	4.57	.94	-	.07	.26**	.22**	-.07	-.06	-.06	-.02
3. Conscientiousness	5.64	.98		-	.34**	.03	.11	-.12*	.06	.06
4. Emotional Stability	5.83	.91			-	.09	.01	.13*	.14*	.17*
5. Openness	4.29	.79				-	-.02	-.29*	-.12*	-.07
6. Blog usage	526.88	1227.96					-	.12*	.23*	.05
7. Twitter usage	1104.54	3616.09						-	.02	.12*
8. Facebook usage	965.48	3173.25							-	.14*
9. Entr. Performance	7.21	2.56								-

[a]. *$p < .05$, **$p < .10$.

[b]. n = 218

4.5 Results

Table 1 shows the correlations examining all dependent and independent variables. Key findings are, firstly, the positive correlations between blog usage with Twitter usage and Facebook usage. Secondly, the correlations between personality traits and social media only show a weak to medium strength. The variables Emotional Stability and Extraversion correlate positively with Twitter usage and Facebook usage, but the variable Openness has a negative sign concerning this correlation. The personal trait Openness negatively correlates with Extraversion, and all other correlations between the Big Five traits that are positive only have a weak to medium strength. Finally, the variable Entrepreneurial Performance is impacted by the entrepreneur's trait Emotional Stability and by Twitter usage and Facebook usage.

Specifically, the influence of personality characteristics is examined on entrepreneur's performance with a latent class regression (Model 1). In addition, isolated influence of social media on performance is investigated (Model 2). The results are reflected in Table 2.

Table 2: Latent Class Regression: Main Effects

	Model 1	Model 2
Constant	1.67**	-.01**
Extraversion	.12*	
Agreeableness	-.07	
Conscientiousness	-.06	
Emotional Stability	.31**	
Openness	-.01	
Blog usage		-.01
Twitter usage		.01*
Facebook usage		.01*
2-log Likelihood	-193.14	-60.41
Overall R^2	.05	.11
BIC	-529.97	-104.36

[a]. ** $p < .05$, * $p < .10$.

[b]. n = 218

Table 2 mainly confirms the results indicated in Table 1. Emotional Stability positively determines Entrepreneurial Performance. Likewise, Twitter usage and Facebook usage impact Entrepreneurial Performance positively on a statistically significant level. In addition, Extraversion also impacts Entrepreneurial Performance positively and is statistically significant. The explained variances are rather low, with 5% and 11% respectively.

Since only Twitter usage and Facebook usage yielded significant results in Table 2, these variables were entered in Table 3 – examining possible mediating effects. Model 1 and 2 test the mediating effect of entrepreneurial traits on the usage of Twitter and Facebook. In Model 1 the mediating effect of entrepreneurial traits can be seen as (a) the effect of Twitter usage loses statistical significance (b) the effect of the variable Emotional Stability becomes larger, (c) the effect of the variable Extraversion achieves statistical significance and becomes stronger, and (d) the effect of the variable Agreeableness reaches statistical significance and becomes stronger. In addition, the explained variance rises to 17%.

In Model 2, the mediating effect of personality traits becomes apparent when looking at (a) the effect of Facebook usage and its loss of statistical significance, (b) the variable Emotional stability and its increased effect strengths, (b) the statistically significant effect of Extraversion, and finally (c) the negative and statistically significant effect of Agreeableness, which becomes apparent only in Model 2. The explained variance increases to 20%.

Table 3: Latent Class Regression: Mediating Effects

	Model 1 (Twitter)	Model 2 (Facebook)
Constant	3.54**	2.91**
Extraversion	.35**	.32**
Agreeableness	-.39**	-.38**
Conscientiousness	.02	-.08
Emotional Stability	.52**	.56**
Openness	.12	.08
Twitter usage	.01	
Facebook usage		.01
2-log Likelihood	-95.92	-72.85
Overall R^2	.17	.20
BIC	-215.30	-143.56

[a]. ** $p < .05$, * $p < .10$.

[b]. n = 218

In Table 3, the moderating effect of the entrepreneur's personal traits on the relationship between social media usage and entrepreneurial performance is tested. For this purpose we multiplied the Big Five with the variables Twitter usage and Facebook usage, resulting in interaction terms for each. As Table 4 justifies, there are no interaction effects except two. The interaction term Agreeableness and Facebook usage achieves statistical significance and has a negative sign. In addition, the interaction term Openness and Facebook usage shows statistical significance and has a positive sign. The explained variance in Model 2 (Facebook usage) achieves 16%. All interaction effects in Model 1 (Twitter usage) are not statistically significant and the explained variance is only 5%.

Table 4: Latent Class Regression: Moderating Effects

	Model 1 (Twitter)	Model 2 (Facebook)
Constant	-.02*	.09**
Extraversion*FB/TW	-.01	.04
Agreeableness*FB/TW	-.00	-.08*
Conscientiousness*FB/TW	.01	-.01
Emotional Stability*FB/TW	-.01	.02
Openness*FB/TW	.00	.05**
2-log Likelihood	-103.34	-73.47
Overall R^2	.05	.16
BIC	-231.85	-146.63

[a]. ** $p < .05$, * $p < .10$.

[b]. n = 218

Our analyses showed that the personal traits of entrepreneurs do indeed have an impact on entrepreneurial performance. However, we only found that Emotional Stability and Extraversion have a direct and positive effect, confirming hypotheses 3 and 5. In addition, our analyses on the direct effects of social media usage reveal that Twitter usage and Facebook usage positively and directly affect entrepreneurial performance, largely confirming hypothesis 6. Therefore, we decided to select these two variables to be tested as mediated by personality traits. Personality traits do indeed mediate the relationship between social media usage and entrepreneurial performance, largely confirming hypothesis 7. The variables Twitter and Facebook usage lose statistical significance, and likewise Agreeableness achieves and Extraversion and Emotional Stability confirm statistical significance. The direct effects of Extraversion and Emotional Stability become even stronger. And finally, after molding interaction terms of all variables with respect to personality and Twitter and Facebook usage respectively, and entering all into to regression models, our analyses shows that there are two moderating effects partly confirming hypothesis 8. Namely, the moderating effects of personality traits Openness and Agreeableness can be found.

4.6 Discussion and Conclusions

The purpose of the present study was to compare the influence of different variables on entrepreneurial performance. We particularly focused on the impact of entrepreneurial traits as an influencing factor between social media usage and the entrepreneur's results. Social media empowers start-up companies not only to communicate with their stakeholders, but also for marketing, recruiting employers, and including customers in developing markets. To this end, including customers in developing markets is indispensable in an increasingly individualized world (Kratzer and Lettl, 2009). Utilizing social media is for most enterprises daily business, particularly in the current sample of Internet and communication technology companies.

At the outset of our investigation we discussed the relationship between certain personality traits and entrepreneurial performance. As our study shows, there is indeed a relationship. But in contrast to Zhao and colleagues (2010), we only found a direct relationship between Extraversion, Emotional Stability, and entrepreneurial performance. Certainly Extraversion and Emotional Stability are of major importance for entrepreneurs in a highly competitive arena with rapid product life cycles, as in Internet and communication technology. In a next step, we were looking at the direct effects of social media usage and entrepreneurial performance. And we found that with the increasing usage of Twitter and Facebook the performance increases. As most of these enterprises can be expected to utilize somehow features of social media, we hypothesized that some personal traits mediate the relationship between social media usage and entrepreneurial performance. And indeed, we find this mediation with respect to Extraversion, Agreeableness (to some degree), and Emotional Stability. Hence, in light of social media usage the personal traits count much more than when considered offline in isolation. This is a first implication that the advent of web 2.0 transfers the visibility and effects of personal traits on entrepreneurial performance into social media, mediating the effect of utilizing social media. Online social networks increasingly substitute offline social networks as platforms for entrepreneurial success. The second implication is that a different portfolio of personal traits as described by Zhao and colleagues (2010) seems to be important. Agreeableness, as a tendency to be pleasant in social situations, was found to be unrelated to performance by Zhao and colleagues (2010). However, when entering this personal trait as mediator, it turns out to a negative determinant of entrepreneurial performance. Thus, particularly in online social networks, Agreeableness may jeopardize business success. It is probable that the negative consequences of showing some potential for being exploited or/and less stable in business competition can cause some negative effects. Agreeableness also shows as interaction term with Facebook usage through its negative consequences on entrepreneurial performance. Another variable, which is statistically significant when entered as mediator, is Extraversion. It is recongnized that the values of Extraversion, such as being sociable, talkative, person-oriented, warm, optimistic and enthusiastic, probably require social media. This might be the reason why Extraversion might have a stronger effect on entrepreneurial performance when having web 2.0 technologies as a catalyst. A third variable which shows mediating a capability is Emotional Stability. Having some rationality in behaving within social media seemingly also has reasonable advantages. Our analyses also revealed Openness to be related to entrepreneurial performance when combined with Facebook usage as interaction term. Being curious and seeking new experiences with a preference for variety might only be propelling the business when an entrepreneur utilizes the information promises of social media. This might also be a trend – to stay abreast of time increasingly requires the utilization of social media for business purposes. Entrepreneurs with a high degree of Openness are not successful on their own without using social media to complement their trait. And finally, Agreeableness also acts as moderator by showing a negative relationship with entrepreneurial performance when entered as interaction term with Facebook usage. Facebook usage may act as a platform for making Agreeableness visible.

The presented results should be interpreted in light of several limitations. With respect to the limitations of a single country study, we suggest that future studies amplify this German sample to an international sample to ensure comparability of results. Second, since social media and the technology around it are very dynamic, a longitudinal research design may be useful. In addition, the study is limited due to potential selection bias of social media. Future research may investigate a broader range of social media platforms. That said, our study is partly exploratory, and as such we avoid drawing explicit predictive or prescriptive conclusions. We hope that future researchers will build upon our work, and work toward drawing more explicit predictive and prescriptive conclusions.

Vita Co-Author Jan Kratzer

Prof. Dr. Jan Kratzer (jan.kratzer@tu-berlin.de) is Chair of Entrepreneurship and Innovation Management and Managing Director of Center for Entrepreneurship at Berlin Institute of Technology, Germany. In addition, he is editor of the Journal of Creativity and Innovation Management (CIM). His research is mainly on factors that drive entrepreneurial activities towards success among others research on networks of entrepreneurs, open innovation networks, social entrepreneurship and online social networks and entrepreneurial opportunities. His work has appeared among more in *Journal of Consumer Research, Economy and Society, Research Policy, Heath Policy, Journal of Product Innovation Management, Research-Technology Management, Technovation, Journal of Mathematical Sociology, Journal of Engineering and Technology Management, International Journal of Project Management, Journal of Small Business and Entrepreneurship, International Journal of Entrepreneurship Venturing.*

Bibliography

Alexa Inc. (2010). Traffic details from Alexa, Retrieved on February 20, 2011, from http://www.alexa.com/siteinfo/twitter.com

Alexa Inc. (2011). Traffic details from Alexa, Retrieved on February 20, 2011, from http://www.alexa.com/siteinfo/facebook.com

Allport, G. W., Odbert, H. S. (1936). Trait Names: A Psycho-Lexical Study. In: Psychological Monographs, Vol. 47, p211.

Amichai-Hamburger, Y. et al. (2002). "On the Internet No One Knows I'm an Introvert": Extraversion, Neuroticism, and Internet Interaction. In: Cyberpsychology & Behavior, Vol. 5, Issue 2, p125-128.

Baer, M. et al. (2008). The Personality Composition of Teams and Creativity: The Moderating Role of Team Creative Confidence. In: Journal of Creative Behavior, Vol. 42, Issue 4, p255-282.

Baron, R.M., Kenny, D.A (1986). The Moderator-Mediator Variable Distinction in Social Psychological Research: Conceptual, Strategic and Statistical Considerations. Journal of Personality Psychology 1986; 51:1173-1182.

Barrick, M. R.; Mount, M. K. (1991). The Big Five Personality Dimensions and Job Performance: A Meta-Analysis. In: Personnel Psychology, Vol. 44, p1-26.

Barrick, M. R. et al. (2001). Personality and Performance at the Beginning of the New Millennium: What Do We Know and Where Do We Go Next? In: International Journal of Selection and Assessment, Vol. 9, p9-30.

Baum, J. R.; Frese, M.; Baron, R. A. (Edt.) (2007). The Psychology of Entrepreneurship. Mahwah, NJ: Erlbaum (The organizational frontiers series).

Bialik, C. (2005). Measuring the Impact of Blogs Requires More Than Counting. In: The Wall Street Journal. Retrieved August 29, 2011, from http://online.wsj.com/public/article/0,,SB111685593903640572,00.html.

Bias, R. G. et al. (2010). An Exploratory Study of Visual and Psychological Correlates of Preference for Onscreen Subpixel-Rendered Text. In: Journal of the American Society for Information Science and Technology, Vol. 61, Issue 4, p745-757.

Block, J. (1995). A Contrarian View of the Five-Factor Approach to Personality Description. In: Psychological Bulletin, Vol. 117, p187-215.

Bouwmeester, S. et al. (2004). Latent Class Regression Analysis for Describing Cognitive Developmental Phenomena: An Application to Transitive Reasoning. European Journal of Developmental Psychology, 1, 67-86.

Brandstätter, H. (1997). Becoming an Entrepreneur - A Question of Personality Structure? In: Journal of Economic Psychology, Vol. 18, p157-177.

Brockhaus, R. H. et al. (1986). The Psychology of the Entrepreneur. In: Sexton, D. L.; Smilor, R. W. (Edt.): The Art and Science of Entrepreneurship. Cambridge, Mass.: Ballinger.

Butt, S., Phillips, J. G. (2008). Personality and Self Reported Mobile Phone Use. In: Computers in Human Behavior, Vol. 24, Issue 2, p346-360.

Cable, D. M., Shane, S. (1997). A Prisoner's Dilemma Approach to Entrepreneur Venture Capitalist Relationships. In: Academy of Management Review, Vol. 22, p142-176.

Carlson, N. (2011). Facebook Has More Than 600 Million Users, Goldman Tells Clients. Retrieved August 29, 2011, from http://www.businessinsider.com/facebook-has-more-than-600-million-users-goldman-tells-clients-2011-1.

Ciavarella, M. A. et al. (2004). The Big Five and Venture Survival: Is There a Linkage? In: Journal of Business Venturing, Vol. 19, p465-483.

Cooper, R. G. (1981). An Empirically Derived New Product Project Selection Model. In: Transactions on Engineering Management, Vol. 28, p54-61.

Corey, L. G. (1971). People Who Claim to Be Opinion Leaders: Identifying Their Characteristics by Self-Report. In: Journal of Marketing, Vol. 34, Issue 4, p48-53.

Correa, T. et al. (2010). Who Interacts on the Web?: The Intersection of Users' Personality and Social Media Use. In: Computers and Human Behavior, Vol. 26, p247-253.

Costa, P. T., McCrae, R. R. (1992). Revised NEO Personality Inventory (NEO-PI-R) and NEO Five Factor Inventory (NEO-FFI) Professional Manual. Odessa: Psychological Assessment Resources.

Costello, K., Hodson, G. (2010). Exploring the Roots of Dehumanization: The Role of Animal-Human Similarity in Promoting Immigrant Humanization. In: Group Processes & Intergroup Relations, Vol. 13, Issue 1, p3-22.

Craig, S., Sorkin A. (2011). Goldman Offering Clients a Chance to Invest in Facebook. Retrieved August 29, 2011, from http://dealbook.nytimes.com/2011/01/02/goldman-invests-in-facebook-at-50-billion-valuation/.

Ebner, W. et al (2005). Blogofy or Die. In: PR Magazin, Issue 12.

Facebook (2011). Press - Statistics. Retrieved August 29, 2011, from http://www.facebook.com/press/info.php?statistics.

Ferris, G. R. et al. (2009). Interaction of Job-Limiting Pain and Political Skill on Job Satisfaction and Organizational Citizenship Behavior. In: Journal of Managerial Psychology, Vol. 24, Issue 7-8, p584-608.

Furnham, A. et al. (2009). Personality, Motivation and Job Satisfaction: Hertzberg Meets the Big Five. In: Journal of Managerial Psychology, Vol. 24, Issue 7-8, p765-779.

Gartner, W. B. (1988). "Who Ss an Entrepreneur?" Is the Wrong Question. In: Entrepreneurship Theory and Practice, Vol. 13, Iusse 4, p47-68.

Gellatly, I. R. (1996). Conscientiousness and Job Performance: Test of a Cognitive Process Model. In: Journal of Applied Psychology, Vol. 81, p474-482.

Geuens, M. et al. (2009). A New Measure of Brand Personality. In: International Journal of Research in Marketing, Vol. 26, Issue 2, p97-107.

Gill, K. (2004). How Can We Measure the Influence of the Blogosphere? Conference 2004. New York. Organisator: WWW2004 conference. Retrieved August 29, 2011, from http://faculty.washington.edu/kegill/pub/www2004_blogosphere_gill.pdf.

Gosling, S. D. et al. (2003). A Very Brief Measure of the Big-Five Personality Domains. In: Journal of Research in Personality, Vol. 37, p504-528.

Grant, A. M., Ashford, S. J. (2008). The Dynamics of Proactivity at Work. In: Research in Organizational Behavior, Vol. 28, p3-34.

Graziano, W. G., Eisenberg, N. (1997). Agreeableness: A Dimension of Personality. In: Hogan, Robert (Edt.): Handbook of personality psychology. San Diego: Academic Press.

Heneman, H. G. (1974). Comparisons of Self and Superior Ratings of Managerial Performance. In: Journal of Applied Psychology, Vol. 59, Issue 5, p638-642.

Hogan, Robert (Edt.) (1997). Handbook of Personality Psychology. San Diego: Academic Press.

Horizont Study (2009). 60 Prozent der deutschen Unternehmen nutzen Social Media. Retrieved August 29, 2011, from http://www.horizont.net/aktuell/digital/pages/protected/Studie-60-Prozent-der-deutschen-Unternehmen-nutzen-Social-Media_88992.html.

Hoyt, C. L. et al. (2009). Choosing the Best (Wo)man for the Job: The Effects of Mortality Salience, Sex, and Gender Stereotypes on Leader Evaluations. In: Leadership Quarterly, Vol. 20, Issue 2, p233-246.

Huffaker, D., Calvert, S. (2005). Gender, Identity and Language Use in Teenage Blogs. In: Journal of Computer-Mediated Communication, Vol. 10, Issue 2. Retrieved August 29, 2011, from http://jcmc.indiana.edu/vol10/issue2/huffaker.html.

Ivcevic, Z., Mayer, J. (2009). Mapping Dimensions of Creativity in the Life-Space. In: Creativity Research Journal, Vol. 21, Issue 2-3, p152-165.

John, O. P., Srivastava, S. (1999). The Big Five Trait Taxonomy: History, Measurement, and Theoretical Perspectives. In: L. A. Pervin; John, O. P. (Edt.): Handbook of Personality: Theory and Research. 2. ed., 3. [print]. New York NY u.a.: Guilford Press, p102-138.

Judge, T. A. et al. (2002). Personality and Leadership: A Qualitative and Quantitative Review. In: Journal of Applied Psychology, Vol. 87, p765-780.

Kaplan, A. M., Haenlein, M. (2010). Users of the World, Unite! The Challenges and Opportunities of Social Media. In: Business Horizons, Vol. 53, p59-68.

Kratzer, J., Lettl, C. (2009). Distinctive Roles of Lead Users and Opinion Leaders in the Social Networks of Schoolchildren. In: Journal of Consumer Research, Vol. 36, p646-659.

L. A. Pervin, John, O. P. (Edt.) (1999). Handbook of Personality: Theory and Research. 2. ed., 3. [print]. New York NY u.a.: Guilford Press.

Landers, R., Lounsbury, J. W. (2006). An Investigation of Big Five and Narrow Personality Traits in Relation to Internet Usage. In: Computers and Human Behavior, Vol. 22, p283-293.

Lee, D. Y., Tsang, E. W. K. (2001). The Effects of Entrepreneurial Personality, Background and Network Activities on Venture Growth. In: Journal of Management Studies, Vol. 38, Issue 4, p583-602.

Li, J., Chignell, M. (2010). Birds of a Feather: How Personality Influences Weblog Writing and Reading. In: International Journal of Human-Computer Studies, Vol. 68, Issue 9, p589-602.

Locke, E. A. et al. (1988). The Determinants of Goal Commitment. In: Academy of Management Review, Vol. 13, Issue 1, p23-39.

Mangold, W. G., Faulds, D. J. (2009). Social Media: The New Hybrid Element of the Promotion Mix. In: Business Horizons, Vol. 52, p357-365.

Markman, G. D., Baron, R. A. (2003). Person-Entrepreneurship Fit: Why Some People Are More Successful As Entrepreneurs Than Others. In: Human Resource Management Review, Vol. 13, p281-301.

Matthews, G. et al. (2008). Personality Traits. 2. ed., 4. print. Cambridge: Cambridge Univ. Press.

Matyka, D. (2011). University paper. Social Media – Temporary Trend or Sustainable Revolution?

Mayer-Uellner, R. (2003). Das Schweigen der Lurker. Politische Partizipation und soziale Kontrolle in Online-Diskussionsforen. München: Fischer(Reinhard).

McCrae, R. R. (1987). Creativity, Divergent Thinking, and Openness to Experience. In: Journal of Personality and Social Psychology, Vol. 52, p1258-1265.

McCrae, R. R., Costa, P. T., JR (1999). A Five-Factor Theory of Personality. In: L. A. Pervin; John, O. P. (Edt.): Handbook of Personality: Theory and Research. 2. ed., 3. [print]. New York NY: Guilford Press, p139-153.

McGann, R. (2004). The Blogosphere By the Numbers. Retrieved August 29, 2011, from www.clickz.com/stats/sectors/traffic_patterns/article.php/3438891.

Miller, C., Sheperd, D. (2004). Blogging As Social Action: A Genre Analysis of the Weblog. Retrieved August 29, 2011, from http://Weblog.lib.umn.edu/blogosphere/blogging_as_social_action_a_genre_analysis_of_the_Weblog.html.

Moeller, E. (2005). Die heimliche Medienrevolution. Wie Weblogs, Wikis und freie Software die Welt verändern. 1. edition, Hannover: Heise (Telepolis Magazin der Netzkultur).

Mooradian, T. et al. (2006). Who Trusts? Personality, Trust and Knowledge Sharing. In: Management Learning, Vol. 37, Issue 4, p523-540.

Morrison, K. A. (1997). How Franchise Job Satisfaction and Personality Affects Performance, Organizational Commitment, Franchisor Relations, and Intention to Remain. In: Journal of Small Business Management, Vol. 35, Issue 3, p39-76.

Motowidlo, S. J., Peterson, N. G. (2008). Effects of Organizational Perspective on Implicit Trait Policies About Correctional Officers' Job Performance. In: Human Performance, Vol. 21, Issue 4, p396-413.

Murphy, G. (1996). Measuring Performance in Entrepreneurship Research. In: Journal of Business Research, Vol. 36, p15-23.

Nicholson, N. et al. (2005). Personality and Domain-Specific Risktaking. In: Journal of Risk Research, Vol. 8, p157-176.

Oreilly, T. (2007). What is Web 2.0: Design Patterns and Business Models for the Next Generation of Software. In: International Journal of Digital Economics, Vol. 65, p17-37.

Poropat, A. E.; Jones, L. (2009). Development and Validation of a Unifactorial Measure of Citizenship Performance. In: Journal of Occupational and Organizational Psychology, Vol. 82, Issue 4, p851-869.

Prebluda, A. (2010. Article on We're Number Two! Facebook Moves Up One Big Spot in the Charts. Retrieved August 29, 2011, from http://Weblog.compete.com/2010/02/17/we%E2%80%99re-number-two-facebook-moves-up-one-big-spot-in-the-charts/.

Quantcast Audience Profile (2010): Twitter Growth. Retrieved August 29, 2011, from http://www.quantcast.com/twitter.com.

Rauch, A., Frese, M. (2007): Born to Be an Entrepreneur? Revisiting the Personality Approach to Entrepreneurship. In: Baum, J. R.; Frese, M.; Baron, R. A. (Edt.): The Psychology of Entrepreneurship. Mahwah, NJ: Erlbaum (The organizational frontiers series), p41-65.

Rentfrow, P. J. et al. (2009). You Are What You Listen To: Young People's Stereotypes About Music Fans. In: Group Processes & Intergroup Relations, Vol. 12, Issue 3, p329-344.

Ross, C. et al. (2009). Personality and Motivations Associated With Facebook Use. In: Computers in Human Behavior, Vol. 25, p578-586.

Rossmann, A. (2010). Web 2.0 Perspektiven für die Marketing & Corporate Communication. Retrieved August 29, 2011, from http://www.competence-site.de/downloads/c4/a9/i_file_276197/web_2.0_perspektiven_fuer_die_marketing_and_corporate_communication.pdf.

Schumpeter, J. A. (1939). BUSINESS CYCLES. A Theoretical, Historical and Statistical Analysis of the Capitalist Process. New York.

Sexton, D. L., Smilor, R. W. (Edt.) (1986). The Art and Science of Entrepreneurship. Cambridge, Mass.: Ballinger.

Stewart, W. H., Roth, P. L. (2001). Risk Propensity Differences Between Entrepreneurs and Managers: A Meta-Analytic Review. In: Journal of Applied Psychology, Vol. 86, Issue 1, p145-153.

Twitter Inc (2009). There Is a List for That. Retrieved August 29, 2011, from http://Weblog.twitter.com/2009/10/theres-list-for-that.html.

van de Garde-Perik, E. et al. (2008). Investigating Privacy Attitudes and Behavior in Relation to Personalization. In: Social Science Computer Review, Vol. 26, Issue 1, p20-43.

Vermunt, J.K, Magidson, J. (2003). Latent Class Models for Classification. Computational Statistics and Data Analysis, 41,3-4, 531-537.

Vermunt, J.K. (2003). Applications of Latent Class Analysis in Social Science Research. Lecture Notes in Artificial Intelligence, 2711, 22-36.

Xia, L. et al. (2009). Exploring Negative Group Dynamics Adversarial Network, Personality, and Performance in Project Groups. In: Management Communication Quarterly, Vol. 23, Issue 1, p32-62.

Zerfaß, A., Boelter, D. (2005). Die neuen Meinungsmacher - Weblogs als Herausforderung für Kampagnen, Marketing, PR und Medien, Nausner & Nausner, Graz.

Zhao, H., Seibert, S. E. (2006). The Big Five Personality Dimensions and Entrepreneurial Status: A Meta-Analytical Review. In: Journal of Applied Psychology, Vol. 91, Issue 2, p259-271.

Zhao, H. et al. (2010). The Relationship of Personality to Entrepreneurial Intentions and Performance: A Meta-Analytic Review. In: Journal of Management, Vol. 36, Issue 2, p381-404.

Der disserta Verlag bietet die kostenlose Publikation
Ihrer Dissertation als hochwertige
Hardcover- oder Paperback-Ausgabe.

Fachautoren bietet der disserta Verlag
die kostenlose Veröffentlichung professioneller Fachbücher.

Der disserta Verlag ist Partner für die Veröffentlichung
von Schriftenreihen aus Hochschule und Wissenschaft.

Weitere Informationen auf www.disserta-verlag.de

www.ingramcontent.com/pod-product-compliance
Lightning Source LLC
Chambersburg PA
CBHW070643300426
44111CB00013B/2238